LIFE BEHIND THE COTTAGE DOOR

LIFE BEHIND THE COTTAGE DOOR

VALERIE PORTER

WHITTET BOOKS

To all my predecessors
in the cottages that have been my homes,
especially at Barnsfold and Kingsham.

And with special thanks to
Emily Lawrence and Maud Bridger.

First published 1992

© 1992 by Valerie Porter

Whittet Books Ltd, 18 Anley Road, London W14 0BY

Design by Paul Saunders

British Library Cataloguing in Publication Data

Porter, Val
    Life Behind the Cottage Door
        I. Title
    307.720942

    ISBN 1-873580-01-0

Typeset by Litho Link Ltd, Welshpool, Powys, Wales
Printed and bound by Bath Press

The author and publishers are grateful to the
following for permission to reproduce the
illustrations on these pages: Mr Chris Howell,
109; Institute of Agricultural History and
Museum of English Rural Life University of
Reading, p. 43, p. 44, p. 48, p. 59, p. 63, p. 82,
p. 96, p. 98, p. 108, p. 109, p. 111, p. 113,
p. 115, p. 121; Ulster Folk and Transport
Museum, p. 104; West Sussex Record Office,
p. 80, p. 87.

CONTENTS

Introduction   8

1. THE FRAMEWORK   16
Materials.   Hearth and home.   Upstairs.   Windows.
Doors.   Floors.   Aspirations.

2. THE DAILY GRIND   40
Cooking.   Lighting.   Storing.   Water.   Washing.
Sanitation.   Rubbish.   Cleaning.

3. THE GREAT OUTDOORS   76
Wildlife.   Backyard beasts.   Cottage gardens.

4. COLOURING THE OUTLINE   93
Furniture and things.   Beds and bedrooms.
Clothes.   Childhood.   Communications

Bibliography   125

Index   127

After Reading in a Letter Proposals for Building a Cottage

Beside a runnel build my shed,
    With stubbles covered o'er;
Let broad oaks o'er its chimney spread,
    And grass-plats grace the door.
        The door may open with a string,
            So that it closes tight;
        And locks would be a wanted thing,
            To keep out thieves at night.
A little garden, not too fine,
    Inclose with painted pales;
And woodbines, round the cot to twine,
    Pin to the wall with nails.
        Let hazels grow, and spindling sedge,
            Bend bowering over-head;
        Dig old man's beard from woodland hedge,
            To twine a summer shade.
Beside the threshold sods provide,
    And build a summer seat;
Plant sweet-briar bushes by its side,
    And flowers that blossom sweet.
        I love the sparrow's ways to watch
            Upon the cotter's sheds,
So here and there pull out the thatch,
        That they may hide their heads.
And as the sweeping swallows stop
    Their flights along the green,
Leave holes within the chimney-top
    To paste their nest between.
        Stick shelves and cupboards round the hut,
            In all the holes and nooks;
        Nor in the corner fail to put
            A cupboard for the books.
Along the floor some sand I'll shift,
    To make it fit to live in;
And then I'll thank ye for the gift,
    As something worth the giving.

JOHN CLARE (1793-1864)

A Wish

Mine be a cot beside the hill;
   A bee-hive's hum shall soothe my ear;
A willowy brook, that turns a mill,
   With many a fall shall linger near.
      The swallow oft beneath my thatch
       Shall twitter from her clay-built nest;
    Oft shall the pilgrim lift the latch
       And share my meal, a welcome guest.
Around my ivied porch shall spring
   Each fragrant flower that drinks the dew;
   And Lucy at her wheel shall sing
     In russet gown and apron blue.

SAMUEL ROGERS (1763-1855)

INTRODUCTION

Two rooms it had, old Bowbrick's cottage, both ten foot square, one down, and one above it approached by a wooden step-ladder through a hole between the joists that supported the gappy planks of the bedroom floor. Neither room had a ceiling, nor more headroom than for a man of modest height. By the turn of the century the cottage had become merely a storage area for the neighbouring village shop and as such it was photographed by the landscape gardener Gertrude Jekyll, who could remember old Bowbrick himself from her childhood in the early 1850s. He wore a patch over his blind eye then, and tied a blue cotton kerchief neatly about his bald head.

In Wormley Wood, some four miles from this little cottage, was an even smaller home of just one room under a thatched roof and it formed a subject for the prolific Victorian artist and London journalist, Helen Allingham, whose watercolours of Surrey cottages have probably tinted many of our misconceptions. Mrs Allingham was a lifelong friend of the children's book illustrator Kate Greenaway and was married to the man who wrote 'Up the airy mountain, down the rushy glen . . .' – and it showed in her work. Like so many Victorians, she sweetened the picture and often posed professional models outside the buildings instead of painting the less comely and far less healthy cottagers themselves.

Mrs Allingham was born in Swadlincote, Derbyshire, in 1848, five years later than Gertrude Jekyll but in the same year as the Wiltshire writer, Richard Jefferies, who in contrast was a countryman in his roots; he was the son of a small farmer and the grandson of a miller, and was considered by his school contemporaries as 'a gentleman's son', who was a little aloof from the local lads. However, Jefferies described in great detail how the genuine old cottages of his time might have been put together by their inhabitants, using whatever materials were to hand, and the word-picture he painted is probably more honest than Mrs Allingham's *Happy England* prettiness. It serves as a reminder that real cottages were often transient by the nature of their materials and crude in their domesticity, even in the second half of the 19th century.

Most of those 'homemade' homes have long since crumbled to dust or been deliberately demolished or so altered that their hearts are invisible. Others, though rarely now, are derelict shells forgotten in remote parts of the country.

Bowbrick's cottage, photographed by Gertrude
Jekyll c.1900.

In a secret, sunlit meadow, sheltered on all sides by oakwoods, I once knew
an old farm cottage so ruined that it could only be rebuilt in the imagination.
It was approached by a mile of rough clay track which in winter and wet
seasons denied access to all but the most determined; thus it had lost its
charm for the practical but increased it for the romantic. In the early 1970s,
when I first knew the place, it was also a mile from the nearest electricity
and mains water supplies and had been unoccupied since a jealous landowner had removed the roof tiles a generation ago to discomfort a family of
post-war squatters. Most of the rafters and floor joists had since
disintegrated or tumbled to the ground; the chimneys and walls were
supported and hidden by a tangle of ivy and brambles so dense that it was
almost impossible to recognize it as a building at all. But you could see how
it must once have been and then dream about who might have lived there a
century or two ago, and how. Even such a skeleton gives a thousand clues
about the everyday life of its long-dead occupants.

Let's call the cottage Songhurst and use it as an example of how cottage-
dwellers can explore the living history of their homes by looking first at the
material evidence on the site and then gradually filling out a picture of how
the cottagers would have lived their daily lives. The principles of

exploration can be applied to any cottage, except that, with those that have been extended and modernized over the years, you will have to strip away (literally or mentally) all the later additions and covering layers until you find the heart of the original building.

One of the joys of cottages (and of the smaller yeoman farmhouses that we now call cottages) is that they were supremely functional. Every part had a practical reason for being there. Question every nook, every hole, every projecting nail, the positioning of the fireplace and the staircase, the level and size of old windows and doors, the traces of soot in unlikely places. Sydney Jones, writing in the 1930s, wrote: 'The requirements of an age seldom outlast its own end . . . Old cottages . . were built many years ago when standards of living were quite different . . . they adequately provided for the modes of domestic life that prevailed when they were built . . . they were just as functional as modern flats are now . . . They fulfilled the requirements of their time by providing for the accepted schemes of human living.' Well, perhaps, though many a cottager of the past would disagree with the word 'adequately'!

Today it might be hard to appreciate the original function but the detective work is all part of the fun of getting to know a cottage and those who lived in it. By understanding the building, you will also come to understand its past occupants and they will be standing at your shoulder, watching and encouraging your search. You owe them a lot.

As you investigate the fabric of the cottage you will glean considerable evidence about the cottagers themselves, even if you have no knowledge of their names. You will discover what materials they used on and in their homes, what their tastes were (where they had the luxury to express them), how they dealt with everyday matters like cooking, sleeping, cleaning, decorating, keeping warm, lighting their rooms, washing and personal hygiene. Let me guide you through Songhurst and show you the way.

Scrambling among the brambles in Songhurst's derelict garden are the rampant growths of those typical double-bloom, mildew-prone, pink and crimson cottage rambler roses; struggling among the forest of self-seeded copse saplings are gnarled old orchard trees with masses of small, sweet fruit; sheltering under the shrubbery are tangled gooseberry bushes; pushing bravely through the long grasses are montbretia and daffodils; straggling over the ivy by a hidden door are determined clumps of the well named everlasting peas whose pinky-purple flowers, though only faintly scented, attract hordes of brimstone butterflies and day-hovering hawkmoths. Even after three or four decades of neglect, this is still a garden and traces of its cultivation will persist for many years yet. Who planted it? What hopes did they have as they pressed the soil comfortably into place against the new roots? Were their dreams realized? If you listen, you will hear.

Over by the yew tree, there is a vigorous forest of nettles – a sure indication of past human settlement. Nettles rapidly colonize farm ditches and old middens, or dungheaps, for example, thriving on the nitrogen from years of enrichment by manure – and the source can be human as well as livestock. This patch, especially near a yew, is probably the site of the cottage's old privy or earth closet.

At the far end of the garden, now under a scrubby woodland of overgrown hedging, squirrels and rabbits have unearthed fragments from the cottage's rubbish pit. Every cottage family had to deal with its own refuse: organic waste went on the compost heap or was burned but indestructible items were buried in shallow pits in the garden or nearby woodland. Unless the wild animals have helped, you will probably only come across a pit by chance when you decide to double-dig a patch of grass as a new vegetable plot, or perhaps when you notice that plants and shrubs never thrive in one part of the garden – and then you discover the endless supply of discarded old batteries buried there, still leaking and crusting after all these years.

Somewhere in the garden, often near a kitchen door, you might catch the slightly dank scent of an old well, long since covered over with boards or stone slabs and now blanketed by undergrowth. You might find evidence of the original well-head – maybe a low, circular wall under the long grass, a couple of rotted posts that once supported a roller for the pail-rope. Songhurst's well is right by its scullery door under a huge paving slab, and I know of one old farmhouse where the well was actually in the big kitchen, under a stone paving slab marked with a 'W'. You might find the dampness of a spring that used to be the only water supply, or the rusted iron of a pump, or a set of steps leading down to the little stream where cottagers used to draw water for washing and drinking – the same stream which might accept the cottage's 'waste-water', as it is euphemistically described.

Now step inside the ruined shell of Songhurst, treading with great care (there are cellars below) while cutting a way through the brambles and saplings that have invaded its old rooms. Ignore the 'front' door in the brick-built part of the place – enter by the wellside doorway where the walls are nothing more than a framework of oak beams.

This is the old scullery or kitchen, though at first glance it could be nothing more than a cartshed. Look for the clues. Immediately to the left of the doorway is what was once the sink (conveniently close to the outside water supply), a sort of brick plinth built against the wall, though there is no sign of the stone sink you might imagine sat on it. Many sinks were in fact of wood and were not designed to hold water but to house water-bowls. Naturally, there was no plumbing. Or this brick plinth might have been the housing for the essential copper, a hefty built-in metal cauldron in which water could be heated by means of its own very small fire hole below. On

11

the opposite wall is a brick oven, projecting outwards between the lean-tos at the back of the building, with its own chimney of crumbling brickwork on the outside.

There are three internal doorways from this central room. To the right, one leads through a partition into a little lobby with a tiny spiral staircase and with access to store-rooms under the delightful sweeps of what can only be described as a catslide outshut – you can still trace something of its flowing lines from the collapsed roof timbers and battens and see that on one wall the roof swept down almost to ground level.

The kitchen-scullery was the original one-room cottage, gradually extended with its series of wrap-around lean-tos which had once housed livestock and a workshop, with access from the outside later blocked off so that the byres became part of the cottage. In the far left-hand corner is a door which opens into a cool, damp cellar, but go carefully here: the steep wooden steps are half-rotten now, turned to dust by countless larvae. The cellars, which do not run under the original cottage, have a couple of high windows (curtained by brambles now) and some slate-topped dairy benches. You can almost smell the cheeses.

In the near left-hand corner the third doorway opens into the extension that was built over the cellar, probably during the 19th century, which turned a humble cottage into a comparatively roomy farmhouse. A straight flight of stairs leads up to its bedrooms but the ruin is too far gone to determine their plan. The old cottage had but a small sleeping-loft under its low-sweeping roof – the one approached by the lobby's tight spiral flight which was in itself an improvement on the original ladder.

The farmhouse extension, forming a T-bar to the cottage, has two good-sized ground floor rooms, each with an end-wall fireplace. In the first of these rooms the fireplace is massive, taking up the whole of the end wall except for its adjoining built-in corner cupboard – it is perhaps three feet deep and eleven feet wide. There is a big baconloft, where the sides of the family pig were smoked and preserved (see p.42), and a broad chimney within (rather than stuck on the outside of the wall) now held up by ivy and briars. The room can be entered direct from the outside by a faded, blue-painted front door standing proudly at the top of two or three steps.

The second room was no doubt the parlour, kept mainly for Victorian visitors, with a modest fireplace and an outside chimney.

The softwood windows in these two rooms are large, three-sectioned casements though only the frames remain now, offering plenty of light and delightful southerly views over the meadow and woods. Those of the original cottage are much smaller and were probably leaded lights at one stage, though in their early history they would have had no glazing at all. The extension is of brick, made from clay dug from the neighbouring pits and probably from the cellar itself – there used to be a small local brickyard here – but the original cottage is a timber-framed building (the site is surrounded by oak woods) with daubed and plastered wattle laths which were apparently never infilled with brick.

All this information can be gleaned from a complete ruin half-hidden by invasive scrub, with no recourse at all to any documentation or local memories – the reading is all in the three-dimensional pages of the site itself. How much easier, then, is it for you to detect the story of your own habitable cottage!

Let me give you another example – a Tudor cottage where my parents have lived for many years. This detective story is a cheat – the building was properly investigated by the local county branch of the Domestic Buildings Research Trust, who interpreted a host of details that I had never even noticed, let alone understood.

Old Pound Cottage, a half-timbered building with a half-hipped tiled roof, has been gently extended over the centuries but was probably first built in the late 16th century as a three-bay house – far too grand to be called a cottage in those days. Bays are typical of timber-framed buildings; each bay serves to divide the length of a house (or barn) on sensible engineering principles by which the structural loads are focused at certain points where they can be supported by major uprights. These substantial posts also support the beams that tie the structure across its span, running between back and front walls, and thus in many cases each bay naturally becomes a room. This was the case at Old Pound Cottage: the original building was a row of three rooms.

At the back is an outshot, running the length of the rooms, and it is clearly an original structure: the back wall of the three bays shows no sign of weathering, so that it has always been protected by the outshot. An outshot or outshut (there are countless other local names for it) is a simple single-storey extension, usually at the back of a small house, under a lean-to or a cat-slide roof, the latter being a pleasing continuation of the downward sweep of the main roof. Outshots were generally intended as service areas such as sculleries, dairies or store rooms, and in later times they were sometimes converted into separate kitchens or bathrooms.

The central bay and the eastern parlour of Old Pound Cottage each used to have a hearth, back to back, and for many years their smoke rose freely from the fires up to a pair of smokehoods fashioned from woven hazel sticks daubed with plaster. Smokehoods pre-date chimneys: they were an early attempt to funnel the fire's pervasive smoke away from the living area. Of wattle or more solid timber, the base of the hood rested on a beam well above the fire and helped to channel the smoke up into the roof, whence it escaped either at random or through deliberately placed outlets. The timber was to some extent protected from fire damage, partly by being well away from the blaze and partly by a coating of plaster, often mixed with cow dung, but many a smokehood succumbed to the flames.

The beam of the parlour's hood in Old Pound Cottage remains in place today just in front of its hearth, resting high on a side wall, and there is a recess for a similar beam in the central hall, though the latter's hearth is now very small. The parlour beam's purpose is betrayed upstairs, where there are grooves for the wattles and mortices of the long-vanished smokehood, and the evidence is even more obvious up in the roof, where there is an area of sooty daub with smoke-blackened rafters alongside.

The research group detected that this system of freely drawn smoke was replaced by brick chimneys in the mid 17th century. The parlour has a square Georgian brick hearth; the third bay was given a small chimney in the 18th century, with a bend in the flue, and the room was divided – the new fireplace was in what is now a small study, while the remaining section accommodated a solid Jacobean oak staircase which made redundant the original stair-ladder next to the old smokehoods.

Above the hearth of the central room is a set of shelves adapted from the old wooden racks across which the iron roasting-spits would have been stored. On the back wall is a huge, heavy oak sideboard which originally folded down against the wall but was later given shelves and drawers to make it a dresser. Beside it is a small, very old built-in cupboard filling what was once an access to the outshot. The front window of this central room has a frame for a slide-up shutter, with two holes in the sill for pegs to hold the shutter up when in place, while one of the parlour windows has diamond-shaped mortice holes for what would have been the bars of an open window. The house was built before glazing became generally available, so that shutters and bars were the only way of keeping out the weather and intruders.

Every floor upstairs has broad, solid old oak boards but the floors swoop and slope at strange angles, sending the unwary sliding. The sloping floors, along with the head-bumpingly low doorways, leaded windows, exposed beams and blacksmith's door latches, give the cottage the character that appeals to many cottage seekers today, however uncomfortable it might be to live in the dream. The place even has a well in front, standing amid a riot of cottage-garden flowers, and a hugely productive orchard of dozens of different old varieties of top fruit and soft fruit at the back.

Old Pound Cottage, delightful though it is, is misnamed. At one time it was indeed the home of a pound-keeper, whose task it was to round up and confine stray livestock until the owners had paid for their release, but he only occupied a part of it, temporarily. The place was built as a whole house, at a time when it would have been fit for quite a substantial farmer or merchant. Although today it is exactly and literally the roses-round-the-door English cottage that many imagine as soon as the word 'cottage' is mentioned, it was far from being a cottage at its inception. Those were the days – and they lasted well into the 18th and 19th centuries – when cottages were one-room hovels built of such transient materials that they were constantly collapsing or succumbing to fire and being replaced by completely new dwellings on the same site.

How did the one-room, smoke-filled hovel become today's desirable residence? And what was life *really* like for cottagers?

— 1 —

THE FRAMEWORK

I will arise and go now, and go to Innisfree,
And a small cabin build there, of clay and wattles made
William Butler Yeats (1865-1939)

THE true cottage began as one room, a shelter from the elements with a roof
and walls made from whatever materials were readily available, with a
sunken floor to save on wall building, to cut down on floor-level draughts
and to provide seating banks. It then gradually developed as needs or
convenience dictated and as standards changed over the centuries but
essentially it remained until the nineteenth century small and simply built,
a refuge largely for those who spent their days working out in all weathers
and needed a few hours under cover in which to rest, eat, thaw out and
procreate.

MATERIALS

The most obvious building materials were earth, stone or timber for the
walls and plant matter for the roof. In an age when the majority worked on
the land (an age which, incidentally, lasted until the 1850s), most rural
homes were quite literally built of mud, sticks and straw. The author Daniel
Defoe (1660-1731) described how some Londoners built themselves rural
shelters which would have been recognized by their early ancestors; it was
after the Plague and they used whatever they could find. 'They made
troughs to sleep in, padded them with leaves, and cut up tent cloth to make
covers.'

In most centuries, people built with whatever they could find close by and it is precisely this use of local materials that gives so much character to old cottages and immediately identifies them with their region. This is really the basis of 'vernacular' building – the use of local materials fashioned by local craftsmen in local styles – and some of us deeply regret its demise by the end of the 19th century when the mass production of building materials, especially brick and tiles, combined with the ease of transporting them by rail all over the country, led to a sameness in every region.

In some regions, the most convenient walling material was stone – such as limestone, sandstone, granite and millstone grit – and the stone cottages of, say, the Cotswolds and Yorkshire are immediately identifiable. In other regions there was ample timber, especially oak, with which to make the framework of a cottage, and plenty of smaller species like hazel and willow to provide sticks woven into wattle panels between the main timbers. If you live in a timber house, you might be able to detect the use of different wood species at different periods, helping to trace the story of the building; it is possible to have the age of a beam checked by, say, dendrochronology (which involves looking at tree-rings) or by radio-carbon dating, but beware: it is easy to be deceived. Many old builders used secondhand materials. Even in the densely wooded oaklands of the Weald, they often preferred to recycle timbers from a shipwreck, which had been thoroughly seasoned and pickled in sea-water, rather than freshly felled local trees. Carpentry styles would be a truer guide to the period of a building's timbers.

Elsewhere, the most obvious material was earth, especially clay for ramming into solid walls or daubing onto wattles or, more laboriously, for greater permanence, baking as bricks. Materials might be combined: flints or pebbles might give body to the walls; stones formed a low-walled foundation for timber frames; chalk gave the basis of plasters to protect the faces of mud walls.

In arable areas and on mixed farms, straw from grain crops was the obvious roofing material; in damper regions reeds and rushes, or on the moors perhaps sprigs of heather, and in some parts oak shingles, birch brushwood or birch bark covered the roof timbers; in a few places the tiles were of stone or slate and in clay areas, eventually, they were of baked clay. Each to their own – every cottage grew out of its immediate environment and remained a part of it while it lived and after it had died, its materials being accepted back again by the earth or being recycled in the building that replaced it on the same site.

I do not intend to go into much architectural or structural detail (the book is concerned more with daily life than with building) but a word or two about mud is relevant. The method of simple building with mud, with or without sticks, is still practised in many countries today and there is much to be said for it. The materials are cheap and to hand; they are easy to

A hovel in Chelsea, c.1800, engraved by J.T. Smith.

shape to suit individual needs and easy enough to repair without the help of architects and professional builders. Wattle and daub is lovely stuff, so versatile and surprisingly long-lasting. It was used as an infill between timbers: pointed vertical poles of a springy wood like hazel were sprung into place between two horizontal timbers already drilled with auger holes and slots for them. Then pliable withy rods were woven among the poles, basket fashion, to make a wattle panel. A pair of such panels would be set, preferably on a low stone foundation, and infilled between them and over them with a mixture of clay-mud, the stuff being added gradually over several months; each layer was trodden down and allowed to dry naturally before another layer was applied. Internal walls might be made of single wattle panels daubed with a mixture of wet clay and horsehair or cowhair or dung, finished off with a coat of plaster on each side. Or outer walls could be built by simply putting up temporary wooden shutters to form walls and ramming down a mixture of earth and straw between them in two-foot layers to make what is called cob, moving the shutters to the next section when the cob was dry and repeating the whole process. To make it more substantial, sticky clay was mixed with chalk and chopped barley straw; Dorset heather, Cornish slate or Devon roadsweepings added to bond the clay, according to local custom; then the building's corners were rounded off so that they were less vulnerable to accidental knocks. Mud could be formed into blocks, dried in the sun, like adobe bricks, and then glued together with mud and rendered or whitewashed for protection. Another variation was to lay courses of turf sods on a stone base, with timbers at the corner for stability, and to top the wall with stones to support the roof timbers.

Building seems to have become so complicated since brick took over. The Romans used fired bricks but the technique was lost in Britain until the Middle Ages, when it was used for grand buildings and gradually spread down to vernacular buildings during the 16th and 17th centuries, making its way across the country until by the second half of the 19th century it had become universal. There were hiccups in its progress: for example a series of brick taxes from 1784 to 1850 ensured that lesser homes only used brick for fireproof chimneys and perhaps for a boastful front, or in stone areas it was combined with local stone for quoins and jambs. After 1850, the combination of mass production of bricks and their transport by rail led to the rapid demise of the local brickworks that had literally given local colour to the material – experts can still tell from what region old bricks came. With luck, you might find a builder from an old local family who can make a pretty good guess at where your bricks were originally dug out from their claypit, assuming they are not mass-produced ones.

(J. T. Smith)

Whatever form the clay might take, raw or baked, plain or strengthened, it could be made more weatherproof by cladding – perhaps with timber clapboarding or vertically-hung tiles to keep rain and frost off the wall material and also to help insulate the building. The lovely, soft-shaped but solid walls of Devon's cob cottages were protected partly by lime-based washes (weatherproofed with animal fat) with a band of pitch painted at the base, and partly by ensuring that the thickness and projection of the thatched roofs threw rainwater well clear of the walls and shielded them to some extent from direct weather.

Thatch was widespread as a material for roofing cottages, be it with straw, reeds, ling or turf. It was cheap, it was available, it was a good insulation. It needed looking after, as the May entry in a poetic farming calendar by Thomas Tusser made clear in the 16th century:

> Where houses be reeded (as houses have need),
> now pare off the moss, and go beat in the reed:
> The juster ye drive it, the smoother and plain,
> more handsome ye make it, to shut off the rain.

The problem he is describing is that the thatch had been lifted by the winter frosts and made loose. The graver problem was that it was far from fireproof and indeed a high proportion of the old cottages burnt down after sparks had set the thatch alight.

Fire was not the only catastrophe – many a mud cottage was demolished by occasional floods or, more deliberately, by a local lord wanting a pleasant view from his country mansion. Most, however, simply disintegrated in the face of the weather. A mere two centuries ago, English cottages in general were not built to last – just like the prefabs of the Second World War. As the 18th century turned into the 19th, the Board of Agriculture drew together county-by-county surveys from England's various agricultural departments and they not only gave details of agricultural practices but also revealed a great deal about each county's rural infrastructure and buildings – including agricultural workers' housing. And a pretty awful picture they painted. The Rev. Arthur Young, reporting on Sussex during the 1790s and early 1800s, said: 'The miserable construction of cottages in many parts of the kingdom, and the too great exclusion of comfort, are circumstances which ought to be remedied. No signs of prosperity like new-built cottages: the dwellings of the poor are, in most counties, but mud-cabbins, with holes that expose the inhabitants to the rigour of the climate. In the Weald of Sussex they are in general warm and comfortable, and many of them built of stone; and on the Downs with flints. Certainly the lower class of people are here in much more eligible circumstances than in many other parts of England which might be named.'

20

(J. T. Smith)

Touring Worcestershire in 1805, Mr W. Pitt found that the labourers'
cottages in general had 'nothing particular to recommend them; in the
ancient villages and common field parishes, they often consist of timber and
plaster walls covered with thatch, and are merely a shelter from the
weather, without any particular attention having been paid to comfort and
convenience, but with the addition of a garden for potatoes and other
vegetables.' They were not all bad – he was impressed with those in the
Bromsgrove parish of Lickey, 'this having been a considerable waste of two
or three thousand acres, a good many cottages had long been erected, and
upon enclosure due attention has been paid to their rights by giving them
an allotment of land.' It was the same in nearby Bourn Heath, where about
twenty cottagers 'now live comfortably on their own premises, with well
cultivated gardens, potatoe grounds, and pigs, but no cows; the cottages are
generally neat and comfortable, many of them new built with brick and tile:

they are, in part, inhabited by farm labourers.' Some had fruit trees too, 'which adds considerably to their comfort', and several were 'very properly built near a perennial stream of clear water, an object of considerable consequence, and which should be always had in view in the erection of cottages, where there is the command of such convenience.' He described in detail a terrace of three little cottages at Lickey, newly built for let, each with 'private lodging rooms' over a kitchen and pantry. They were all supplied by the same pump and there was a communal room for washing and baking. They were relatively robust, too: the outer walls were only one brick thick (lengthways) and the inside ones but half a brick thick, but at least they were of brick, and had plastered walls, tiled roofs, brick floors, glazed windows and upstairs floorboards of elm on oak timbers.

The situation in Devon in the 1790s was surveyed by Charles Vancouver who grew quite apoplectic. The old and venerable mansions of the county, he said, were generally built in stone, which was 'variously dispersed, and by no means difficult to procure' in most parts of the county. 'This would', he said sternly, 'have been thought sufficient to have caused a discontinuance of the use of mud-walls; it has not, however, produced that effect, as the cob buildings are nearly as numerous as is presumed to have been the case with the Belgae, who, we are told, were the first who made inroads and established colonies in Devonshire. Garden-walls, farm-houses, barns, stables, linneys, village fences, and cottages, are all built with this dull, heavy, and deforming material . . . without rough-cast, or white-wash to conceal the native colour of the loam.' He admitted that cob cottages could be made clean and comfortable if they *were* rough-cast and whitewashed, and that for about sixty pounds one could be built with a fireplace and oven in a principal room about 14 feet square, with two small rooms behind for fuel and provisions, and the upper storey divided into two apartments, one for the parents and one for the children. But in many places there was an acute shortage of cottages, and yet existing ones had been allowed to fall into ruins or were grossly crowded. Here and there landlords made an effort: Lord Clifford was praised for building 'very neat cottages' for his workmen, 'the window in the upper story is so placed, as to admit light to the two rooms into which this floor is divided,' added Vancouver with pleased surprise, and each had a small garden 'with the privilege of cultivating as many potatoes as their industry may prompt, or leisure admit of,' along with a small orchard 'sufficient to produce from one to two hogsheads of cider, with a sufficiency of good hoarding or winter apples . . . in lieu of the grazing of a cow, which they were formerly indulged with. The cow being subject to accident, places this munificence on a more permanent footing.' But then he reached Chilworthy, 'where three mud walls and a hedge-bank form the habitation of many of the peasantry.'

In the same district, the Reverend Luxmore had built a row of a dozen

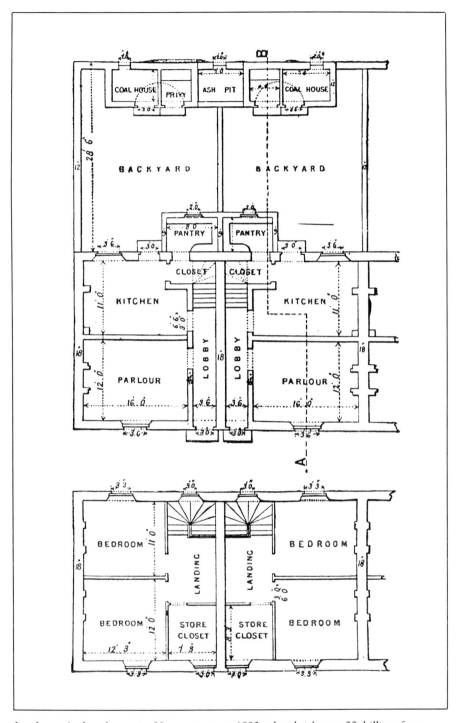

Landowner's plans for a pair of farm cottages, c.1890, when bricks cost 20 shillings for a thousand (in *Youatt's Complete Grazier*).

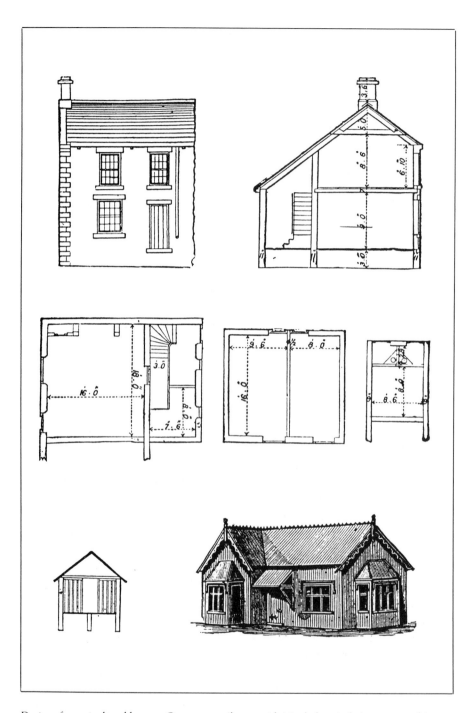

Designs for agricultural homes. One cottage (*bottom right*) is clad entirely in corrugated iron, lined with wood inside. 'In the thaw following a severe frost', explained the original caption, 'the water from the melted ice beneath the roof is liable to find its way through the fissures in the matchboard of the ceiling.' (in *Youatt's Complete Grazier*).

new cottages in the village of Bridestow: each had a downstairs room 16 feet square with a door and a window in the front, a fireplace (with an oven opening into it), a door to a back shed or lean-to for fuel, tools and the cottage pig (with another door leading out into a back yard). Under the stairs in the front room was a pantry; opposite the mantle-pieced fireplace was a dresser fixed to the wall, with shelves. The bedroom was the same size as the living-room below. The cottage walls were of stone, 20 inches thick, up to 8 feet high; the superstructure of cob (with straw mixed into the clay) was as thick and was 'covered with a slate room'. The floor of the main room was lime-ash, and that of the bedroom had boards of 'rack deal, or any soft wood plank most convenient to be procured'. From this fine home, let for a shilling a week, tenants ran the risk of being evicted instantly by the Reverend if they were 'disorderly'; they must also 'frequent the church, and behave themselves soberly, and carefully, and as good neighbours to each other.'

In another part of Devon, Vancouver noted with concern that the cottages and farmhouses tended to be 'crowded together in villages' rather than scattered on the farms. 'The morals of the peasantry are thus more liable to be corrupted, than in more detached and solitary situations, where they would have much greater conveniences in garden-ground, so essential to the comforts and necessities of the peasant family.' In another district, where the cottages were 'in a state of alarming decrease', Lord Rolle was encouraging people to leave the village and settle on the borders of common land, and Vancouver said approvingly that this would not only promote their comfort but also improve their morals. Each was allowed an acre at first, and if they improved their patch to his lordship's satisfaction they would be granted more acres – up to five. 'In thus withdrawing the cottager from his former haunts in the village,' explained Vancouver, 'the time that would otherwise be spent at the ale-house, or in frivolous conversation with his neighbours, is now employed to the immediate benefit of himself and family, and ultimately to the increase of the national stock.' And this was long before Queen Victoria came to the throne!

It was not until the 18th and 19th centuries that the more permanent building materials began to filter right down to cottage level. This 'filtering' of materials and styles is typical in the story of cottages: very broadly, fashions spread downwards through social levels and geographically from the Continent to the south-east and thence fanning out across the rest of the country, but the pace of the spread, from both sources, could be very slow indeed and it could be literally half a century or more before a cottage in, say, the north-west began to show features which had become commonplace in cottages of the south-east. Cottage-dating is a minefield for the unwary.

Most of what we now call cottages were not originally cottages at all but the more substantially built homes of yeoman farmers, merchants, clergymen and those of similar social and economic standing. Real cottages were very small and very crowded – and very smoky inside.

HEARTH AND HOME

'Fire is a capital article,' wrote William Cobbett in his *Cottage Economy* notes addressed to the 'Labouring Classes of this Kingdom' in 1823. 'To have no fire, or a bad fire, to sit by, is a most dismal thing. In such a state man and wife must be something out of the common way to be in good humour with each other, to say nothing of colds, and other ailments which are the natural consequence of such misery. If we suppose the great Creator to condescend to survey his works in detail, what object can be so pleasing to him as that of the labourer, after his return from the toils of a cold winter day, sitting with his wife and children round a cheerful fire, while the wind whistles in the chimney and the rain pelts the roof? But, of all God's creation what is so miserable to behold or to think of as a wretched, half-starved family creeping to their nest of flocks or straw, there to lie shivering, till sent forth by the fear of absolutely expiring from want?'

Fire is a magnet that has always drawn the human eye to its warmth and

The central hearth, 19th century: cooking pot, home-smoked kippers, and 'wind-eyes' in the eaves.

supplied the focus of tribal and home life all over the world. It is ironic that, today, its place has been usurped by the cold, flickering light of the remotely generated pictures from a television set in the corner. What a contrast to the liveliness of the flames and their scope for imagination! In Dickens's *Our Mutual Friend*, Lizzie Hexam saw countless images in those dancing tongues and glowing, crackling embers. 'Of an evening, Charley,' she told her young brother, 'when you are at the school . . . Then as I sit a-looking at the fire, I seem to see in the burning coal – like where that glow is now –' and, as Charley takes up the poker, 'Don't disturb it, Charley, or it'll be all in a blaze. It's that dull glow near it, coming and going, that I mean. When I look at it of an evening, it comes like pictures to me, Charley.' But when Charley asks to be shown where to look for the picture, she tells him that it wants *her* eyes to see it all. And later she sees a hollow in the fire where she used to see Charley's image, and she knows what must be done.

Fire has been so central to domestic life that it is almost as if homes were originally built to envelop and protect a fragment of the tribal campfire for each family – a roof to prevent the rain from dousing the flames, and walls to embrace and contain their warmth. The hearth was the heart of the home until the latter half of the 20th century, and the house developed around it and was dominated by it.

The word 'hearth' essentially means the part of the ground or floor on which a fire is habitually lit. At first it was literally that – a patch on the earth floor in the middle of the room, with no means of drawing the smoke away. Then it was given a stone base – the hearthstone – or perhaps a clay one, depending on what was locally available. But it remained a campfire, an open fire, its smoke drifting freely and gradually finding an escape route through gaps in the thatch or through small holes deliberately made high in the roof – there were no ceilings to impede it. Small cottages were chronically smoky inside and no doubt lung cancer would have claimed many a life had not diseases caused by appalling sanitation got there first. It is important to remember that smoke problem, as it determined several design stages in cottage architecture and furnishings – for example, chairs were low so that the sitters had some chance of being below the accumulated smoke level, and for a long while it was the smoke that deterred the development of upper-storey sleeping areas – the open roof was the smokiest part of the cottage. So the family lived on the ground floor, at fire level, and would sit, eat and sleep all in the same room.

The fire provided evening light as well as warmth and it also retained a strong element of superstition, or religion if you prefer the word. Many cottagers saw it as important to keep the fire burning continuously, day and night, whatever the season – partly for its warmth and light, partly to save the bother of re-lighting it in times when matches had not been invented, but partly from a subconscious feeling that it was unlucky to let the main fire die, a feeling fed by the old tradition that a squatter who could build a shanty and have a fire going within it before sunrise had the right to remain there. The fire represented hope, defiance and life and even today I know of countless older cottagers who keep their solid-fuel Rayburns warm all year round, regarding them very much as the heart of the home, the familiar friend that greets them when they come home and is still welcoming when they rise in the morning.

Very gradually, the hearth became more sophisticated and more permanent in its structure, with a few basic improvements filtering down as ideas from superior buildings, such as deliberately placed smoke outlets in the roof or upper parts of the wall in the form of louvres which, in theory, could be manipulated according to the direction of the wind, or simply small openings that did their best to draw out the smoke at random. Later came canopies to catch some of the smoke and then a backscreen which in due course became a partition dividing the room in two.

When hearths were moved to be against the wall (by the 16th century in most parts), hoods of wattle panels daubed with clay and plaster served to gather the smoke. Finally people began to build more solid chimney flues from stone or, preferably, brick. These became almost universal from the 18th century onwards, in mansion and in cottage, but cottagers, already tight for indoor space, tacked their chimneys on to the outside of the wall – which was not only space-saving but also a way of boasting that you could afford a chimney!

Cottage in Middlesex, 1790s (J.T. Smith).

UPSTAIRS

It was not until the smoke was at last captured by hood or chimney that the cottager could sleep in comparative comfort upstairs. The first stage in two-storey development was to lay a few planks across one end of the room at head height, using the tops of the walls for crossbeam rests (the walls, of course, rose only to the eaves, which came down to head level). Access to this new sleeping platform was by means of a ladder – like old Bowbrick's cottage in the 1850s and like many a lesser house in the early 18th century – or a staircase steep enough to be more at home on a ship as a companionway. Next came space-saving spiral steps, either beside the new chimney or in a turret added to the outside wall. Staircases of straight flights needed space – and head height too – but they gradually became more common, especially the more compact dog-legs doubling back on themselves, though there was still the problem of low eaves, which meant that staircases tended to be central, under the highest part of the roof – the very space so often taken up by the chimney that had become the core of the larger cottage.

Gradually the sleeping loft, a partial area over one end of a communal room, led in due course to the whole of the ground floor being divided from

An early loft conversion: sleeping loft in a Yorkshire cottage (Drawing by Sydney R. Jones in *Old English Household Life*, 1925).

the open rafters of the roof by the wooden planks that were the floor of the upper storey. In new buildings, or when old ones needed re-roofing, the outside walls were continued upwards to create a proper upstairs, rather than an attic, giving more headroom. The bedroom floor planks were merely laid across the wall-to-wall beams and with good gaps between them to save timber, so that privacy was negligible and draughts were free to whistle where they would. It was a while before the downstairs rooms were given a ceiling under the joists – at first plastering was applied directly to the underside of the floorboards, if at all. The upstairs rooms remained open to the rafters and to all that might care to drop from the roof, like rodents and insects and thatch dust and bird-droppings and rainwater . . . Today, insulated, we no longer share our homes with nature.

So, gradually, the cottage progressed and became by degrees more comfortable to live in – and more introverted. There were drawbacks to such progress, however, and one of them was that it was no longer so easy for the family to build its own shelter. Building became a craft and a trade, and it became necessary to pay experienced builders to do the work instead of doing it yourself. The occupants began to lose control – they submitted to others' designs and techniques and, in due course, others' standards. A century ago the first local government councils came into being and it was not long before there were planning departments to say whether or not you could build at all, and building inspectors to make sure you did it all 'properly'. The cottage no longer reflected the idiosyncrasies of its own inhabitants' tastes and needs.

Richard Jefferies was born (and died) before local councils took such a commanding role. Living from 1848 to 1887, he described in detail how a man might set about building his very own cottage with the help of a few good friends. It had a good-sized living-room with a fireplace and chimney, a lean-to housing a baking oven, and a downstairs bedroom; the walls rose to just a little above head height and were whitewashed; the thatched roof had no ceiling; the floor was of earth. And even in this Victorian period, such a cottage was far from being considered a hovel at a time when many still lived surrounded by wattle panels daubed with mud. Jefferies's cottage builder did the work himself, with the help or advice of experienced locals, and might be more ambitious by adding an upstairs storey as well as taking a pride in making a good garden, hedged with quick-growing elder until he could set something thicker, with a little gate or two fashioned from sticks.

Two centuries earlier, some of Defoe's post-plague Londoners had built something almost as good: a carpenter 'in a few days built a shed and later a house, with rafters and roof, and an upper floor where they lodged warm. It was thatched and the walls made of earth were thick. Against the earth wall at one end they made a chimney, and with a deal of trouble fitted it with a funnel, to carry off the smoak . . . and constructed a hearth with a hollow so that they could bake bread.' Such homemade homes were being put up in the forests and on common land by a generation relieved to have survived the plague and determined to make the best of their precious lives by living off the land, well away from the crowds.

Cottages can be full of surprises and frequently deceive later generations. In the Lincolnshire village of Bratoft, for example, a very ordinary though very small house with red brick walls and scruffy grey roof tiles had been the home since 1914 of Nellie Padley, a self-sufficient woman living off the land there until 1979. During the 1980s, while the walls were being patched up, someone discovered that there was a secret cottage within, hidden by Nellie in a jacket of brick and tile as a practical attempt to make the place warmer and drier. Under the tiles, screened inside by chipboard, was an excellent thatched roof; between the brick walls and the thick, interior wallpaper were the well preserved mud-and-stud walls of the original 18th-century cottage. The little place had a hearth at the heart of its two downstairs rooms, each no more than six feet wide and less than six feet high, with two similarly tiny rooms above up a flight of nine steps. It had been built by squatters, probably in a matter of two or three days, and its fire still burns continuously to honour the byelaws that, at the time of its building, allowed the squatters to remain once they had lit their first fire on the hearth.

Those squatters were typical of the many thousands who usually settled on strips of manorial waste along the lanes, fashioning cottages out of the cheapest possible materials but fashioning them to suit personal needs and managing to create homes with far more character than the precise edifices made by 'proper' builders. They might have been humble hovels and shanties but their creators took a pride in their ability to put a roof over their own heads and some, like Nellie Padley's, have defiantly survived the centuries. They are cottages with heart.

WINDOWS

'Window': think about the word. It means 'wind eye'. Go back to that one-room hut with its open central fire and all the smoke. Back then, the hut was a place in which people passed only the dark hours – the hours when they were not working out of doors – or perhaps the impossibly cold or wet days now and then. The hut provided shelter and warmth and its inhabitants were either asleep or were gathered around the light and heat of the fire to eat. They did not need other 'lights' from openings in the wall apart from the doorway; they had no glass and those openings would only have admitted the weather. But they did need escape holes for the smoke. The most obvious outlet might seem a hole in the roof but that, too, would admit the elements and drown the fire. The answer was a hole or two near the top of the walls.

In the Tudor cottage described in the Introduction, there was evidence of the original windows created before glazing was generally available. Even grand houses rarely had glass in their windows before the late 16th century (when that cottage was built) and the openings were therefore as small as possible. They repelled intruders by means of lattices – perhaps criss-crossed wooden laths or sticks, or wickerwork, or in superior houses stone mullions. They admitted light and fresh air but they also admitted wind and rain. There was not much of a deterrent for the entry of wildlife, either, but then, people were used to sharing their homes with mice and moths, bats and beetles . . .

The Tudor cottage, you will remember, showed evidence of a system of wooden shutters which could be pulled up to keep out the weather or the intruders. They stood on the floor when not in use and were then slid upwards to cover the window, and pegged into position. Indoor shutters were quite common, more often sliding than hinged.

Early materials for keeping out nature but admitting at least a little light included parchment and thin, translucent layers of cattle horn, though the latter was in such small sections that it was usually reserved for horn-paned lanterns. Waxed linen or coarse sacking were alternatives – especially the latter for cottage window coverings. The next stage was glazing. At first, glass was blown in the form of thin, mottled discs: a blob of molten glass on the end of a stem was twirled so that it flattened into a disc, the centrifugal force forming it into ripples like those from a stone dropped into a pond; the stem was cut off, leaving a thick-middled whorled circle which shaded to thinner areas towards the edges. The thin edges formed the best glass and the thick middles were sold off cheap to cottagers. They were cut into the necessary shapes and then set as small pieces in the lattices – very small pieces, little better than horn, whose size made framing them quite tricky. The problem was solved by using soft lead strips to grip the pieces of glass; then these leaded networks could be wired to an iron frame to make the whole thing rigid.

Glass-making and window-framing techniques gradually improved and by the late 17th century smaller houses were often glazed. However, many cottages continued with their old sack-covered holes until the 19th century, when plate glass (as opposed to spun glass) was first made in quantity and cut into larger panes. At last, after about 1840, the quality of glass was more uniform, but if you have any early Victorian glass in your cottage you will still see signs of the slight waviness of the old spun glass. By the middle of that century glass had become much cheaper and of a quality which allowed the use of larger window panes. Simultaneously came the

Slats protect the unglazed window openings of a one-room cottage, 18th century (J.T. Smith).

ending of the window taxes which had existed from 1697 until 1851; at that stage, though some cottages were glazed, many still made do with paper windows. My own Victorian farm cottage still had cardboard in its windows in the mid 20th century, not to mention chickens in the main room and barn owls in the bedroom.

Stained glass crept into the suburbs on a wave of arty craftiness from about 1860, reaching a peak under the influence of art nouveau before the Great War, but it did not filter down to many of the humbler cottages. Its presence usually indicates that a cottage was snapped up by a town-dweller escaping the rat-race.

The early windows were not designed to open. If you wanted ventilation, you did without glass or you left the door open or you found your fresh air outside. Indoors, in contrast to the all-weather fields in which you probably worked, was *supposed* to be fuggy. It was not until perhaps the mid 18th century that cottage windows could be opened, either on side-hung hinges or as sashes which slid horizontally rather than vertically. But by then many cottages had only one very small opening section within a fixed window – perhaps no more than a single pane. Vertically sliding sashes came over from the Continent early in the 18th century but did not begin to filter down to cottages for many decades – cottagers seemed to prefer their casements.

Curtains? No – blinds used less material. It was not until Victorian times that curtains became more usual in small houses and even then cottagers could rarely afford such a luxury.

DOORS

In the venerable Sussex town of Petworth, tucked into the huge, dominating shadows of the high stone boundary walls of Petworth House, a little row of old stone cottages makes you wonder about the stature of the previous generations of cottagers. The doors on to the street here are scarcely four feet high. Were people really so small when the cottages were built? Or did they enter at a crouch, like eskimos? Were they deliberately built low to deter intruders as in days of yore when, in theory, an unwanted visitor, bending to enter, would inevitably come head-first into the room and could be easily decapitated? Hmm. Apparently the present generation of Japanese has so outgrown its parents that architects have had to revise all their measurements upwards very suddenly, especially for ceilings (by twelve inches) and doors.

At first, doors were not hinged or fixed in any way. They were simply propped in place when necessary and lifted away when not. The doors of a cottage I lived in during the '70s could be lifted off their farm-gate-like hinges and set aside when required, rather like the old Irish system of having only one wooden door in the cottage which was lifted off and put over a different doorway when the wind changed direction. Indeed, wooden doors were something of a luxury. More common in cottages were homemade panels, perhaps of wattle hurdles or brushwood propped in the gap, or woven mats of rushes and straw supported from top hooks or on straw hinges, or at worst no more than a piece of sacking hanging like a curtain. Proper timber doors, with metal or wooden hinges, were for better-class houses and the old makeshift ones lasted in some places throughout the 19th century, a time when those cottages that did have doors also began to have iron locks and bolts. But many retain homemade and often very clever wooden latches, with fingerholes and levers and toggled strings in all sorts of ingenious personal designs.

FLOORS

The old cottages were built directly onto the ground, and earth formed the floor of many a cottage even in the 19th century – earth which had been raked about and thoroughly watered to make mud, which was then dried and beaten with flat pieces of wood until it was as smooth and hard as leather. The method was broadly similar to puddling clay as a pond lining. When the floor began to show signs of wear, it could be patched with fresh clay or, if the surface had become unbearably rough, the whole floor could be dug up and the neighbours invited in for a floor-trampling party. Sometimes strengthening materials were added, especially fragments of bone; you could make lattice patterns by setting pigs-trotter bones (flattened by cutting or rubbing into two-inch squares) into the ground and filling in the squares with the small bones from sheep's legs, rammed down a few inches deep into the mud and laid knuckle uppermost. Or you could give the floor a gleaming hard finish either by mixing ox blood with fine clay or by washing the surface with sooty water, though the mere act of regular sweeping was often enough to give a reasonable surface. Or you could use a superior mixture of rammed lime and ash, creating a sort of plaster floor.

Earth floors were economical but they had many drawbacks. They became natural dustbins; Erasmus, the Dutch humanist who moved to England in 1498, described the state of English homes in lurid detail and claimed that people simply chucked their food-bones and beer dregs on the floor to mingle with 'spittle and vomit and urine of dogs . . . and other filth unmentionable' that became trapped in a festering layer under the rushes strewn over the earth. The rushes (or bracken or straw) served other purposes than a carpet under which to sweep things; they were soft and warm underfoot, they could easily be renewed, and they helped to some extent to lay the earth dust, though they themselves created plenty as they crumbled with age, and they were a considerable hazard near an open fire.

Most beaten-earth floors were dusty, of course. The dust rose with every tread or scuff of a foot, with every opening of the door, with every passing draught (and these were many). It settled everywhere. Recently an American couple who had 'dropped out' to live in an earth-floored cabin in a remote part of their state were the subject of a television documentary; one of the most enduring images from that programme was the thick layer of dust that covered every shelf, every piece of furniture and every book within half a day.

The simplest way to lay the dust was to sprinkle the floor and its rushes with water. This was often done for you by nature, especially in the many cases where the floor was below ground level and the doorway admitted rainwater run-off from outside. I know of several old cottages even today whose sunken floors flood with depressing regularity in rainy seasons and in one of them the flooding sometimes comes from the garden cesspit.

Where the materials were locally available, cottagers began to lay more durable and cleanable floors of stone, slate or baked clay tiles and bricks – and very cold these surfaces could be. They were also very damp, drawing up moisture from the unprotected earth beneath them and sweating in certain weather conditions. At first they were only used for heavy-duty areas like the threshold and around the hearth, and sometimes the stones were carefully decorated by the housewife. She might simply rub them to a gleaming cleanness with a lump of whiting (ground chalk) or use some yellowish 'Flanders brick' to colour them. She might embellish the cleaned stone by darkening it with milk and drawing patterns with light-coloured sandstone or a dried ball of white clay, or daub the hearth with a rag dipped in a damp mixture of pipeclay or 'potmould' to make spots, or she might use a sharp piece of pipeclay to draw squares and then decorate their centres with simple flower forms. Or she might dampen the stones and then sprinkle them with coloured sand, brushed into swirling patterns. For a brick floor, those who could afford it might buy special floor-sand or sawdust and sprinkle it afresh each week in a fine layer, to keep the floor more dry, but such a luxury was usually reserved for the farmhouse kitchen unless there was a free local source there for the taking.

Then came floorboards and very occasionally an inspired cottager might paint them in a favourite colour or, more rarely, paint patterns on them. However, hardwood planks were expensive and it was not until imported 'deal' (a general term for softwood timber) became more available from the 18th century onwards that cottagers could afford to lay close-boarded floors upstairs instead of gappy planks or rush-bedded plaster or simply layers of birch faggots. It was even later before they could afford to lay boards downstairs as well.

The next stage was to cover the downstairs boards or paving with floor cloths in better cottages, though few could afford such an extravagance until very late in Victoria's reign – floor coverings of any kind were unusual even in grand houses until the 19th century and tended to derive from table covers (which originally included carpets). Floor cloths might be of canvas painted with pigmented linseed oil, or later printed, and they were neither cheap enough nor durable enough for cottage use. Cottagers might replace their loose rushes with old potato sacks or home-woven mats made from rushes, grass or plaited straw; they might even laboriously weave a hard-wearing mat or two from horse hair.

Most cottagers, however, made rag rugs and continued to do so during the 20th century, hooking strips cut from old clothing through a sacking backcloth or weaving longer rag strips as if making cloth. You simply cut up all your old skirts, coats and flannel items and unstitched a new sack to make the backing. They cost nothing to make and were warm and soft underfoot – and colourful, too. They would be scattered where they were most needed, especially by the hearth and (oh, luxury!) beside the bed. Jumble sales are a modern thing – rags were far too useful to be given away, though neighbours would pass their clothes on to each other and of course children wore hand-me-downs. With luck a village child born after the Great War might be given one new summer dress and perhaps one jumper and skirt or trousers given by their Sunday school teacher, maybe, or by the manor house. Someone would probably knit them a jumper and stockings as a Christmas present – and there would be no other presents at all. New clothes were worn for Sundays, and Sundays only; the next best were school clothes and the oldest clothes were worn for playing or helping in the house and garden. Cottagers had the habit, ingrained by generations of low income, of wasting absolutely nothing and they excelled in the art of mending and recycling everything that came their way.

In the 1860s someone invented linoleum, which was in effect reinforced floorcloth, its pigmented linseed oil having been mixed with cork grindings, and this would become the cottager's wall-to-wall carpet. Proper carpets remained far out of reach for cottagers until a long way into the 20th century, despite the mass production of them by the factories during the 19th and despite the so-called 'Scotch carpet', the cheapest type, being in theory affordable. The Scottish landscape gardener John Claudius Loudon (1783-1843), who published an *Encyclopaedia of Cottage, Farm and Villa Architecture* in 1836, had a somewhat romantic idea of cottages: he suggested that cottagers should use loose carpets in their bedrooms and parlours, turning them at intervals for equal wear (eight turns in all, including flipping these unbacked carpets over). He also suggested that strips of carpet could be laid on the floor around the bed and beside the 'dressing-table' (a thoroughly middle-class piece of furniture for a cottager, especially in the time of dire rural poverty in which his book was published) and said that no cottage should be without its stair carpet. Perhaps his theories applied more to the fashionable *cottage ornée* built as a charming rural retreat for those who could afford such things.

ASPIRATIONS

Parlours were rare in genuine old cottages, which usually had just one general living-room. The parlour was a Victorian invention which met the needs of those who aspired to climb the social ladder and was particularly a feature of farmhouses in the period when farmers began to consider their wives as household managers rather than equal partners in farm labour.

However, by the end of the 19th century parlours were also a great source of pride to cottage women, who felt even more heartened if their home had a hall as well. Council houses, the first of which were being built very soon after local councils came into being in the late 1880s and early 1890s, were eagerly sought after because they often had a hall, albeit no more than a tiny lobby, as much as because they had mod cons and were new and clean. Parlours and halls gave cottagers an increased sense of self-respect as well as extra space and, in the case of the hall, some preservation from the pervasive front-door draughts. One should never mock the cottagers' aspirations: most of them certainly earned what little dignity they could achieve. Writing in the late 1930s, for example, Barbara Wilcox described the typically deceptive Rose Cottage inhabited by one Mrs Coles. It was a whitewashed and half-timbered cottage with eyebrow windows in its thatch, stone-flagged floors, a splendid inglenook fireplace, a tiny spiral staircase to two bedrooms with minute, floor-level windows. Mrs Coles soon disabused her visitor of the romance of the cottage. Damp spread through the cracks of the old stone flags, laid straight on to the earth beneath; the front door (opening into the kitchen) was so badly fitted in its frame that it was less draughty left open than closed; the scullery outhouse had a copper but no sink and certainly no hot water, except from the kitchen fire's kettle, and no drainage – slops were thrown into the garden; the inglenook fire had been fitted with a kitchen range but, like the original, it smoked violently unless the window was left open; the walls were soaking wet with damp, summer and winter, which had rotted the plaster and which defied the occupants' cover-ups with numerous layers of paper; the stair treads were so dangerously rotten that you had to trust your weight only to the very edge of the treads; the teeny bedroom windows had only one little pane which could be opened and you could only stand upright in the centre of the room, avoiding the slope of the roof.

Mrs Coles had done her best with her awkward cottage – it was as clean as she could make it and there were cheerful curtains at the windows, a very clean counterpane over the bed, a big central table in the main room covered with a chenille cloth and supporting a plant in a pot wrapped with pink tissue paper. The walls bore countless pictures, mostly of royalty or of famous British victories, hunting scenes and maidens attended by cavaliers, with a selection of children in nightwear gazing heavenwards at angels. But Mrs Coles despaired of the place – after all, she was living in the late 1930s, not the 19th century – and was thrilled to be moving into a brand new, brick-built council semi with, oh joy!, a hall. She was immensely proud, too, of its tiny parlour, with its dark paint and buff wallpaper – it was an unnecessary room and that was why it was so desirable. The kitchen was well enough designed to have windows at either end for good ventilation (she would stick paper over the draught cracks) and had a range which in theory would also *heat the water*. And there were cupboards; there was a scullery with a sink, a water-closet, a bath in its own alcove and a copper. And there were three bedrooms, all separate – no more walking through one to reach another. Oh bliss! Who needed cottages when they had the chance of council houses? Who needed 'character' and charm when they could have relative comfort and convenience?

— 2 —

THE
DAILY GRIND

THE old fireplaces against the screen or wall were huge – big enough to take large, long logs (why waste energy by cutting them smaller?) and bulky stumps or roots. The wood might be simply laid on the hearthstone, or suspended across iron fire-dogs so that there was a little draught underneath to encourage burning. The better off might protect the fireplace bricks from cracking in the heat by installing iron fire-backs, often with a design of an oak tree or something vaguely heraldic, and it was thought that these also helped to reflect heat into the room, though in fact fire-proof bricks could have acted as heat-stores.

These big inglenook fireplaces were deep and wide enough for people to sit within them and escape the constant cold draughts that were part of cottage life. There was a substantial oak beam across the front at a height which meant you needed to duck to reach your cosy fireside bench, and there was usually a strip of material hanging from it to regulate the chimney's draw – perhaps some sacking or a little curtain of printed cotton or red, corded moreen.

COOKING

The fireplace's chimney was cavernous and usually had a wooden (yes, wooden in cottages) bar about six or seven feet above the fire so that the big iron cooking pot could be suspended over the flames. The height of a hanger, hooked over the bar, could be adjusted by a simple ratchet device and the pot itself hung by its handle from the ratchet's hooked tip. This 'chimney crane' could also support the kettle, or a cheese-making cauldron, or any other vessel which had a handle over the top. Sometimes the fire-dogs supported a couple of square-section iron bars, laid loose across them, which could easily be sited so that they supported a pot just above the hot embers. Some fire-dogs were tall enough to support a meat-roasting spit at the back, or were 'cup-dogs' with adjustable iron cup holders on their front uprights for warming mulled ale. Metal ale-mullers were also sometimes slipper-shaped so that the 'foot' could be pushed right into the embers.

Spits might be simple iron rods, perhaps stored across a carved spit-rack above the mantelshelf when not in use, adding to the fireplace ornaments and other things stored there for convenience and decoration, such as pepper pots and horn mugs, or even a keeper's gun. There might be a more elaborate basket-spit, which surrounded a bigger joint of meat, or a strong double-pronged spit; both of these could be turned automatically by a smokejack – a tin vane propelled by the fire's strong updraught to rotate the spit by means of various gears and pulleys. The better off could play with quite a variety of ingenious spit-turners and during the 19th century many

Sitting in the inglenook. The iron cooking pot is hanging from a bar within the chimney.

homes used 'bottle-jacks' (so named for their shape). Poorer cottagers improvised with twisted string or took their precious joint of meat to the village baker's oven, while many people actually preferred to roast their meat outside over a bonfire, weather permitting. Roasting needed a hotter fire than the traditionally slow-simmering pot and you can imagine that such a blaze would make a small cottage overpoweringly hot.

Farm wives had baked their own bread for several generations in built-in brick ovens shaped like beehives: they were fired by burning faggots (bundles of brushwood) which were then removed and the brickwork retained the heat. Cottagers could not usually afford such installations but in some parts of the country they used portable 'cloam' ovens made of earthenware – especially in Devon and Cornwall. Many a Devon cottage had the mouth of its oven opening into the chimney, which made feeding the fire rather inconvenient. Elsewhere they improvised by turning the iron cooking pot upside down over what was to be baked and heaping hot ashes around it on the open fire, or built a separate baking oven outside.

Home baking declined quite rapidly in 19th century cottages: it was easier to take your dough down to the village oven or to buy your loaves from the village baker. Many bakers operated public baking days when people could bring not only their bread dough, cakes and buns but also their puddings and roasting joints to be cooked centrally, which was a great saving in fuel at home. This practice probably reached its peak during the depressed 1920s (at a penny a time) in an age when the majority still had no more than an open fire with a side oven for cooking.

Most farmhouses, and many a well built cottage, had space in the substantial chimney to hang sides of bacon from the family pig so that they could be smoked after they had been salt-cured. Some homes had built-in baconlofts. These were almost little rooms in themselves within the chimney breast, which remained broad enough to accommodate them. In most cases, the loft had iron bars arching across it, as high as a man could reach, bearing hooks on which the bacon flitches were hung to absorb woodsmoke (always oak) for several weeks. Smaller hams hung from iron hooks driven into the loft's wall. The loft had its own ceiling to keep the rain away and its own floor or ledge to prevent the bacon juices from falling into the fire below.

In our own time, those hidden baconloft ledges can be a trap for the unwary. I lived in a small, isolated Georgian farm cottage which, one Christmas Eve, developed an inglenook chimney fire so severe that the fire brigade had to be summoned. They eventually discovered the seat of the fire after breaking into the central chimney through a bedroom wall too hot to touch: lo, there was a long-forgotten baconloft which had been accumulating soot and birdsnest debris for goodness knows how many decades.

The smoking of bacon could be quite a complicated business, though more often than not it was left to chance. Cobbett gave very detailed advice in his *Cottage Economy* tracts (1823) for those who probably had no proper loft but simply hung their bacon in the chimney. First, he said, the flitches must be hung where no rain could fall upon them, and secondly they must not 'be so near the fire as to *melt*'. The smoke must be from a wood fire but not a coniferous wood, and the fire must be a constant one for about a month. 'But,' he admonished, 'over-smoking, or rather, too long hanging in the air, makes the bacon *rust* . . . The flitch ought not to be dried up to the hardness of a board, and yet it ought to be perfectly dry. Before you hang it up, lay it on the floor, scatter the flesh-side pretty thickly over with bran, or with some fine saw-dust other than that of deal or fir. Rub it on the flesh, or pat it well down upon it. This keeps the smoke from getting into the little openings, and makes a sort of crust to be dried on; and, in short, keeps the flesh cleaner than it would otherwise be.' And after all that, you might still run the risk of 'nasty things that they call *hoppers*; that is to say, a sort of skipping maggots, engendered by a fly which has a great relish for bacon.' To prevent this unpleasantness, it seems that the Americans smoked only the pig's hams, and they covered these with coarse linen 'such as the finest hop-bags are made of', neatly sewn in place. Then they painted the cloth all over with a lime whitewash – the same as was used to paint walls. Five layers of such a wash, each layer being allowed to dry in the sun before the next was applied, could apparently deter any fly. The English method, however, was to put some sifted, clean, dry wood-ashes in the bottom of a box, lay a flitch on them, cover it in more ashes, lay the second flitch on top (pigs have two sides!) and then finish off with a layer of ashes up to eight inches deep. '*Dust*,' said Cobbett, 'or even *sand*, very, very *dry*, would, perhaps, do as well,' the object being to exclude not only the flies but also air. The cottager who took such precautions would find that 'the bacon will be as good at the end of the year as on the first day; and it will keep two and even three years perfectly good.' Bacon, claimed Cobbett, 'is the great thing. It is always ready; as good cold as hot; goes to the field or the coppices conveniently; in harvest and other busy times demands the pot to be boiled only on a Sunday; has twice as much strength in it as any other thing of the same weight; and, in short, has in it every quality that tends to make a labourer's family able to work and well off. One pound of bacon . . . is worth four or five of ordinary mutton or beef . . . But always observe, it is *fat bacon* that I am talking about; . . . *old lean bacon* is not good.' With or without the protective ashes or sand!

The cooking pot itself took pride of place. It was a hefty cast-iron thing, usually oval in shape, and made to last several lifetimes. Before the 18th century, though, cauldrons were usually made of a copper alloy known as bell metal, which probably poisoned many a family over the years since it also contained lead and zinc. But a new smelting process led to the mass production of affordable and increasingly convenient iron pots, at first comfortably pot-bellied with two little 'ear' handles near the rim for holding and a pail-like handle between them for hanging. In due course they were given flat, legless bases to stand on the 19th century's new range hobs.

Boiling, or rather simmering slowly, was the main cooking method and whole meals were boiled in the family pot – a favourite method of cooking for some three thousand years in Britain which persisted to some extent into the 20th century. Cottagers who are today in their seventies can remember the routine and the delicious flavour of meat pervading the vegetables and pudding – some of them find separately cooked vegetables completely tasteless in comparison. Emily Lawrence, a good friend of mine who has lived in the village all her life, described to me just how her grandmother used to prepare the boil-in-a-pot meal. She would save the cotton bags in which shops supplied rice, flour and sugar and would boil them to get out the dye (usually the shop's name). Then she would put the bacon joint into the pot, full of boiling water, and cook it for a while; next, she would tie the vegetables into a cotton bag and the potatoes into another cotton bag and

Cottage clutter: wicker bird cage on wooden settle, woman's pattens and man's boots, besom, flat-irons, skillets and trivets, iron pipe-racks and, by the stump, a working man's tools – reed comb, fencing-post mall, dibbing iron and (on the mantelshelf) a pair of police constable's rattles used as bird-scarers in the crop field.

44

add them to the pot along with a suet pudding tied up in some white cloth – probably a piece of worn-out sheet. The meal would be transferred to hot dishes when everything was ready to eat – bacon, vegetables, potatoes and *half* the suet pudding. The other half was eaten as a jam and treacle rolypoly for 'afters'. There is nothing new about boil-in-the-bag . . .

Every cottage also had its collection of skillets, again quite weighty, in brass, bronze or earthenware, with long saucepan-type handles so that they could be put on the fire from a safe distance. They either had three legs moulded to the body or could be set into a separate three-legged trivet. Other iron trivets, with their own handles, had surfaces on which all sorts of cooking vessels could be stood safely and it was these that supported the flat-bottomed saucepans that replaced skillets after the 18th century. There might be an iron frying pan with a very long handle, though boiling, stewing and roasting were far more common cooking methods, and there might be one or two small baking irons, which were iron plates with curved handles, standing on their dumpy little legs on the hearth among the hot ashes to bake small items. Flat pans like these had been used for many centuries, over campfires as well as indoor hearths, as hot plates for baking griddle cakes and also to keep food warm.

There were all sorts of iron implements – toasting forks (sometimes attached by springs to a stand in such a way that their height could easily be adjusted), curved irons for raking baked potatoes out from the ashes, assorted tongs (including small 'brand tongs' so that you could light your pipe – or candle – by picking up a piece of hot ember), and pokers and shovels and perhaps a pair of leather-and-wood bellows. No wonder the blacksmith was such an important person in every village.

(*Left*) Trivets.

(*Below*) Three-legged cooking pot, obtainable in various sizes and priced according to capacity – from sixpence three-farthings for the two-pint size, up to half a crown for the four-gallon pot.

The kettle was often hung on an idle-back – a lever that enabled you to pour hot water from it without actually touching the kettle itself. Its hanger, like the pot's, was ratcheted so that you could adjust its position over the fire and, if you were very lucky and good friends with the blacksmith, you might have a complicated chimney crane rather than a mere pot-bar. It would have an iron hanging arm which could be pivoted away from the fire when you wanted to attend to the pot or kettle without singeing yourself.

Unlike pots, many kettles were made from sheets of brass, copper or tin rather than cast in a piece. The sheets were formed into more-or-less straight-sided receptacles, usually oval or oblong in shape. The main difference between the pot and the kettle was that the latter had a close-fitting lid and was originally used for boiling hams or fish. It did not, however, have a spout until the 18th century, when tea-drinking began to spread down through the social levels and there was a demand for constant hot water for brewing up. Some were given dinky little brass taps near the base instead of pouring spouts.

Fuel for the open hearth was whatever was handy – mainly wood or, in treeless areas, peat, turf or dried dung (still an important fuel today in some parts of the world). Emily, like many other cottagers (including myself), still collects wood on every walk by habit and remembers how children would spend their Saturdays going along hedgerows and into the woods to bring back sticks. Many agricultural and estate workers were allowed to take fallen wood such as oak boughs and nobody ever walked anywhere without keeping an eye open for something burnable, including deadwood in the hedges, fir cones and discarded brushwood. The ashes from wood fires were carefully saved: they could be used for making lye for laundry work or mixed with fat to make soap.

In some parts of the country by the mid 17th century, coal was increasingly used by cottagers wherever this fossilized form of wood could be mined, though in other areas coal did not become standard fuel until the canals and, especially, the railways made its transportation in bulk easy and cheap. Coal fires, unlike log fires, needed grates to burn efficiently and these became common with the spread of coal. By then, all but the humblest of cottages had chimneys and had developed wallside fireplaces.

The fireplace became an increasingly sophisticated cooking area and during the 19th century it also became much smaller as its chimney flues and grates became more efficient, until it was no longer possible to huddle within the inglenook on its built-in seats or three-legged stools, as had been the custom when most of the heat had floated straight up the chimney. And you could not help but be aware of that chimney: its huge, cavernous mouth was wide open and you could, if the fire was ever out for long enough, look up inside it and see the sky . . . see the daytime starlings and the night-time owls perching on its top, their conversations and hoots floating down into the room as if they were in there with you. No wonder the draught came howling down. But at least such a chimney, broad and straight, was easy enough to clean: you simply rammed a holly branch up and down, or (some claim) dropped an irate hen down from the top so that her agitated flapping and scrabbling did the job in no time. I have known the occasional jackdaw do the same by mistake, bringing down not only a pile of soot but also large amounts of nesting debris.

It was largely coal that made the development of smaller, less draughty fireplaces possible and gradually builders began to work out how to avoid smoky rooms by narrowing the chimney throat to improve the draw. The scientist Count Rumford in the 18th century devised the basic principles that improved many a smoky inglenook flue: in essence he reduced the throat of the fireplace to 4 inches wide and 6 to 8 inches deep, perpendicularly over the fire, with smooth surfaces for all the smoke passages, especially at the entrance to the throat, which was rounded under the front arch. He added a smoke shelf, horizontal and level with the top of the throat, about 6 to 8 inches above the top of the fireplace opening, and he gave the fireplace splayed sides, the width at the back being about one third of that at the open front. There was also a need for sufficient depth from the chimney breast face to the back of the fireplace to prevent smoking caused by draughts across the opening of the fireplace. Or at least that was the ideal. There was also the problem of chimney height, surrounding trees and goodness knows what else: chimney building and fireplace design are tricky arts.

Next came the realization that a great deal of lost heat could be saved if it was reflected back into the room by redesigning the fireplace and its opening. For a long while the latter had been square but during the mid 19th century arched openings became all the rage. Then came a fashion for lining the grate with firebricks, which retained heat better than the old iron fire-backs, and during the 1870s came the slow burning grate on a solid fire-brick base, acting much like a storage heater and leading to rectangular openings surrounded by glazed tiles and tiled hearths, with adjustable metal canopies that helped to direct the smoke and control the draw.

These now very small fireplaces were efficient for heating a room but no good at all for cooking and to most country cottagers they were a fancy luxury for those who had parlours and could afford the fuel for more than one fire at a time. Cottage life remained centred about the multi-purpose open hearth that provided a cooking place as well as warmth in what could truly be described as the living-room – a place in which people cooked and chatted and worked and relaxed and sometimes still slept, a room which in larger homes such as farmhouses was the kitchen.

By the second half of the 18th century, iron founders and blacksmiths were making fireplace accessories like cast-iron hobs and iron baking ovens so that the kitchen's open fireplace was developing into an open 'range' – which is to say that it offered a range of facilities: warmth, baking and boiling, all from a single fire source. Through most of the 19th century (and in many places during much of the 20th as well), the typical cottage kitchen in areas where coal was readily available had a combined range with an open fire in the centre heating an iron oven on one side and a boiler on the other, both with hobs on top for pans and kettles but also with cranes so

Open coal range with oven on one side and boiler on the other.

that the utensils could be hung above the flames and meat could still be roasted over an open fire. A built-in boiler was something of a luxury in cottages, however, and many continued the old system of boiling their water in big iron or copper vessels which had to be lifted on to the fire. Of course, built-in range boilers had no plumbing at first – they had to be filled by hand from the top and emptied in the same way unless they were fitted with an outlet tap.

Where wood remained the traditional fuel (in southern England, for example) many cottagers continued to cook over an open fire inside those big chimneys, either hanging their vessels from the bar over the fire or resting them on trivets, roasting meat on spits over the flames and smoking bacon up the chimney. Whatever the fuel, most cottagers kept a stockpot simmering constantly over the fire, its quiet steam drifting with the fire smoke, until the later Victorians ruined this comforting image by starting up soup-kitchens for down-and-outs, so that people began to equate soup with charity and extreme poverty.

The advantage of the open range was that it cooked food, it heated the room and it also gave you flames to look at and gather around – but it was not very efficient and, as ever, most of the heat still vanished up the chimney. And if the original fireplace had smoked, so did the open range – so much so that many cottagers had to keep at least a window open whenever the fire was burning.

During the 19th century came the next kitchen development – the closed range, which burned the same fuels far more efficiently so that you used less and retained more of the heat. The fire was contained under a cast-iron cover (which was also a hotplate) so that smoke and soot were kept away from food and pans. But many continued to prefer an open fire for roasting their joints (as all barbecuers will appreciate) and found that oven-roasting in the new ranges often produced nasty results until techniques evolved which allowed air to circulate within the oven. However, the oven could be used for other things – like airing your clean laundry or warming your vest or drying out your boots . . .

Mary French, describing life in her Cornish village of Quethiock up to 1919, said that farm kitchens all retained their traditional open fireplaces,

Mass-produced range 'with Hot Closet and Open and Close Fire'. This is Young & Marten's *Delight*, fitted with 'Patent Raising Bottom Grate'. Prices from 57 shillings (£2.35 in today's currency).

49

with cloam baking ovens (started by using hot ashes from the open fire to light the oven faggots) in a chimney recess beside them, but by 1919 some also had iron kitchen ranges on the other side of the fireplace for quick baking. A few also had stoves. The ovens were only lit once a week, on baking day, but the open fire was always at least quietly glowing as the focal point of the whole farmhouse.

Most cottagers liked it even less when, in the interests of creating a stronger draught for a hotter oven, iron founders began to add doors at the front of the fire. English cottagers (and farmers) liked to see their flames in all their glory, which is one reason why they never really took to the free-standing iron stoves that became so popular on the Continent and in America. Nor did they like having to learn fiddly techniques in operating dampers for different situations on the closed ranges. And of course they were expensive to install: they had to be built into the brickwork, and the flue had to be cleaned frequently and regularly checked for blockages (oh, those blessed starlings and jackdaws . . .)

The Victorian *Larbert* cooking range.

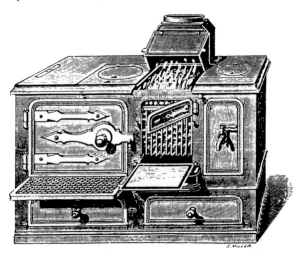

Anthracite, a much cleaner fuel which burned so slowly that the fire could easily be kept in all night, was in theory ideal for cottage ranges but in practice it was too expensive to buy. In 1929 the first Aga cookers came into Britain from Sweden but, again, they were far too expensive for cottagers, though they were snapped up for farmhouse kitchens. However, many cottagers eventually installed the cheaper, friendlier little Rayburns which fitted so neatly into the kitchen's old open fireplace. By then, though, solid fuels were already beginning to lose the battle against new, cleaner and much more responsive sources of domestic energy – gas and electricity. How much simpler cooking, heating and lighting became – but they took a while to reach rural areas. Piped gas was for towns, not the countryside (and that is still the case for most of us), though butane was available in containers by the Second World War, while mains electricity did not reach most rural areas until the 1950s, even in the home counties. Some are still waiting for it today; some, however, were offered its advantages between the wars, even as early as the '20s, but the older cottagers rejected it in spite of the electricity board's offer of a free cooker and three light switches. Electric cookers simply did not have the heart – they could not be the comfortable focus of cottage life, their instant heat was dangerous for the unwary used to hours of careful stoking to bring up the cooking temperature, and some even claimed that food cooked on the electric tasted of nothing and had no nutritional value at all.

During the 20th century cottagers also cooked on oil stoves, with an elaborate network of oil-filled, burbling pipes and a tendency to become pretty filthy. They could be temperamental, and if you failed to keep the top clean after greasy cooking the flames mightly suddenly swirl into life in the tide of a draught and set light to the caked fat. Many women hated and feared them, though in theory they were economical and easily regulated, but you had to be very careful to keep the wick clean and properly trimmed to avoid that flaring up which led to a sooty, smutty kitchen or something much worse.

Others can remember the wonderfully energy-efficient hay-box, a simple wooden box packed tightly with hay, with a hole in the middle for a casserole pot. The meal was initially heated by other means – say quarter of an hour in an oven – and then transferred to the hay-box for the rest of its cooking. A thick pad of hay on top of the pot ensured that it was completely insulated and the food continued to cook slowly for several hours – perfect for stews and porridge and casseroles, and using very little fuel indeed.

Meanwhile the pots and pans were changing too. Copper, so laborious to clean and so dangerous if in contact with acid fruits or vinegar during the cooking, had long since given way to iron, a heavy, serviceable and almost non-stick material. But iron had a tendency to rust and the vessels were given a plating of tin inside, which had a habit of melting or wearing off. The next development was enamelling on the inside of iron vessels and soon everything was enamelled – saucepans, water jugs, kettles, bowls and all. Enamelware could be mended at home if necessary: you bought pot-menders at the village shop – two pieces of tin with a bit of cork – and you screwed them through the hole, or you made use of the travelling tinkers. Then came aluminium, which was very light compared with iron and did not rust, but the cheaper aluminium pans were thin and liable to buckle with the heat, nor could they be cleaned with soda, the favourite grease-fighter. During the 1930s, stainless steel and fireproof glass and earthenware gradually found their way into the cottage kitchen and both cooking and cleaning became easier and safer as a result.

LIGHTING

Light, other than daylight and firelight, was not a priority until a cottager (usually a woman) had to rely on home-based piecework to eke out abysmally low agricultural wages. She would work well into the night to earn a penny or two after many hours of eye-straining work such as lace-making or glove-stitching. Artificial light was such a luxury that women would share it: they gathered in groups in each other's cottages to share warmth and company as well as a single candle whose gleam was enhanced and dispersed by shining through glass globes filled with water.

Candles were beyond the means of most, even in the 19th century. As Cobbett said in the 1820s, 'We are not permitted to make Candles ourselves, and, if we were, they ought seldom to be used in a labourer's family. I was bred and brought up mostly by *Rush-light*, and I do not find that I see less clearly than other people. Candles certainly were not much used in English labourer's dwellings in the days when they had meat dinners and Sunday coats. Potatoes and taxed candles seem to have grown into fashion together; and, perhaps, for this reason: that, when the pot ceased to afford *grease* for the rushes, the potatoe-gorger was compelled to go to the chandler's shop for light to swallow the potatoes by, else he might have devoured peeling and all.' Cobbett considered potatoes to be the source of all sorts of evils!

In rural areas they made their own light sources from wild rushes gathered in the summer meadows when fully grown but still green. True rushes have a pithy core, a delicate aerated network which looks vaguely like foam rubber. To make the light, you cut off both ends of the rush so that it was perhaps 18 inches long and carefully peeled away all but a narrow, supportive vertical strip of the rush's green rind and hung it up to dry in bunches. Then you laid a dozen at a time in a three-legged, boat-shaped, cast-iron dish (a grisset) containing melted grease – preferably mutton fat, if you could afford it, as it dried harder than beef fat. If you were really poor you might have to use pig fat but your rushlight's smoke would be foully black and smelly.

You drew the rushes through the melted grease, letting them soak it up, and then left them to dry on a piece of young tree-bark nailed to the beam or strapped to the wall. You could carry your rushlight in your hand or use a rushlight holder, which had a sort of crocodile clip – a spring-held iron gripper like delicate pliers, with a knob or curled counterweight to keep the jaws gently closed on the rush. Village smiths produced hundreds of their own designs but they were usually fairly simple and lodged into a wooden base so that they could stand on a table or shelf. There were also taller floor-standing models and, later, some rushlight holders also had a socket for homemade candles (still based on rushes for wicks but dipped in grease time and time again, drying between coats until they built up a good thickness). The candles were kept in special boxes made of sheet iron or tinplate because the tallow quickly became rancid if left out in the air.

Rushlights were set between their jaws at an angle with about an inch and a half protruding, with a rag or scrap of paper under the long end of the rush to stop grease dripping on the table. Then it was lit and had to be shifted forward in its holder at frequent intervals to expose more 'wick'. A rush about 15 inches long could give you half an hour of admittedly weak light with good management. To douse it, you crossed two pins through the rush or you took a burning length of rush to bed and laid it on the edge of the chest while you undressed. When the lit portion reached the wood, it extinguished itself – and usually left a little burnt groove in the edge of the furniture.

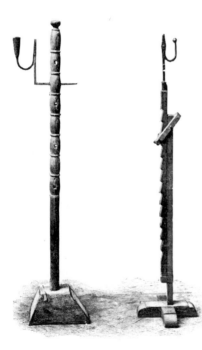

Rushlight holders with wooden floor stand. Both are adjustable for height: the stand on the left is pierced with holes to accept the iron holder; the one on the right has a ratchet device.

Rushlights were all that most cottagers could afford, though some could not – they were only cheap if you had the meat to supply the grease, and very often that fat was desperately needed as fuel for the human body, which was far more important than being able to see at night – and remained all they could afford until the mid 19th century. Cobbett praised them highly, claiming they gave a better light than the common small dip-candle. 'You may do any sort of work by this light,' he advised, 'and, if reading be your taste, you may read the foul libels, the lies and abuse, which are circulated gratis about *me* by the "Society for promoting *Christian knowledge*", as well by rush-light as you can by the light of taxed candles.'

Meanwhile candle-making was improved by the use of cotton wicks instead of rushes but the rendering of the tallow was a smelly business at the best of times. Tallow is animal fat, and at that period it was so vital (for human energy and for light) that livestock were deliberately bred and fed to produce as much fat as possible – a strong contrast to today. 'Mutton' fat, incidentally, came from goats as well as sheep.

Candlesticks, for those who could run to candles, were for a long time made of iron. An early design was a spiral of strap iron which could cleverly be used to adjust the height as the candle burned down. Another typical style was shaped rather like a smoking pipe and had a spike so that it could be driven into a beam or a mortar joint. Plain iron pillar-shaped candlesticks for the kitchen were still in use when Gertrude Jekyll was writing about cottage life at the turn of the century and she described many ingenious devices such as extendable jointed arms or hanging ratchets for

Spiral strap-iron candlesticks for simple height adjustment.

candle-holders. More cherished than practical iron were the brass candlesticks which graced even cottage mantelpieces and were passed down as heirlooms.

During the 19th century, candles began to be mass-produced. Some were still tapering tallow dips but others were uniformly shaped in moulds, like household candles today. A still familiar name from that period is Price – E.

Price & Company began to make coconut-oil candles in 1830 and from then on led the candle-making field in Britain, developing improved wicks and refined fats. In 1857 another chandler introduced mineral-based candles made of paraffin wax distilled from oil shales and this led to the production of cheap but good quality candles – something that had been out of reach of those who could not afford expensive beeswax or spermeceti (made from spermwhale oil). Now the candle industry was really booming but candles were still too precious to be wasted by cottagers. Emily Lawrence remembers when candles were the family's main source of light, even when paraffin became more widely available. They had just one paraffin lamp, with a globe over the flame (spare lamp glasses and the paraffin could be bought at the village store), and they needed lots of wick. It was essential to keep the lamp clean – it became charred during the evening and the wick was clipped with scissors very carefully, as if just a speck was left on the end the glass would be smeared with smoke. The lamp was refilled daily and was kept permanently in the main room, so that everybody took a candle with them when they left that room to go to bed, or to go down the garden to the toilet, or even to go to church. Out of doors you carried your precious candle in a glass-sided holder (an improvement on horn lanterns) so that it did not blow out but it had air holes at the top and you tried to cover them with your hand to make sure you were not suddenly plunged into darkness. Indoor candlesticks were usually of metal, sometimes of china and, as a luxury, of brass.

And how did you light your rush or your candle, then? Well, usually from the ever-burning open fire but even that sometimes grew cold. Every cottage had its round, sheet-metal tinderbox, often with its own candle socket in the lid. Inside there was a fragment of flint, shaped with a comfy thumb-hollow and with a blunt striking edge, and there was a 'steel' – perhaps an old file. There were some sulphur matches – thin slivers of wood about three inches long, their points at both ends dipped in melted brimstone. There was a disc, loosely fitted, with a ring-handle on top, which was the damper for extinguishing the final component of striking a light – the tinder under the disc. This was bits of rags – old scraps of cotton and linen. The technique (and it was an art indeed) was to hold the steel in one hand, the flint in the other, and strike them together until a spark fell on to the tinder in the box. Then you could blow gently and, with luck, manage to light your match from it. (Sometimes it took a smidgeon of gunpowder to get things going!) Then you quenched the tinder with the damper disc.

Lucifer matches, tipped with phosphorus and sold by the gross, were first imported from France in the 1830s, when they were known as Congreves. But matches remained precious for many decades and Emily remembers keeping them in a metal box to make sure that they did not catch fire by mistake – to save using them, she would fold a piece of paper and light it from the fire.

Next time there is a power cut, just think back to how difficult it used to be to strike a light – no wonder people went to bed with the sun. It was certainly not just a flick of a switch to get light or warmth or cooking power. It became easier when lamp-oils, paraffin and gas became available – country cottagers were beginning to use paraffin from the mid 19th century and George Dew noted in his diary in November, 1874, that his household had set up 'two spirit lamps for burning Benzoline, a mineral spirit' instead of candles and that these would be cleaner, lighter and cheaper.

STORING

Think again about power cuts. They deprive you not only of light but also of cold – refrigeration. Although the first refrigerators were made in the United States in 1845, fridges have only become cottage furniture within the last three or four decades at most, partly because of the lack of mains electricity before the late '40s and early '50s in rural areas, partly because of their capital cost, and partly because cottagers had traditional methods of food storage such as salting, smoking, pickling, preserving and fermenting, otherwise eating fresh food only when it was in season and while it was still fresh enough not to need refrigeration anyway.

Meat, generally something of a luxury, was kept in a cool place. The larder (and dairy, if there was such a thing) faced north and was furnished with cool slate slabs and a flyproof meatsafe with perforated-metal sides exposed to the outside air. Jugs of milk were also kept in the meatsafe, covered with pieces of material weighted in place with beads along the edges, and the meat was sometimes dusted with pepper as an extra precaution against flies.

Home-reared pig meat was the staple. When its time came, the animal was butchered into its many usable parts and, as usual, nothing was wasted – offal, brains, blood, trotters as well as hams and sides of bacon and sausage meat and pork. Very little was eaten fresh and it was important to preserve most for the winter months, when a worker's body needed plenty of edible fat for energy and internal warmth. So the cottagers cured hams in brine and hung bacon sides as high up in the chimney as they could reach so that the meat would be smoked by the wood-burning fire but not scorched by its flames. Other flesh could also be smoked, especially fish in seaside villages, and even mutton, though this was not particularly liked.

Salt was a great preservative for vegetables, too, and I still have a huge earthenware jar given to me long ago by an old farmer for salting green beans. You put salt in first, then a layer of beans, then salt and more beans and so on. The next day the beans would have sunk so you added some more – you wanted to exclude as much air as possible. The salt drew the bean juices and created a brine solution, which needed to be right to the top of the jar before it was covered with an airtight lid. Salt was a precious commodity and was stored in a dry place – usually near the range or in its own cupboard in the inglenook.

Fruit was bottled to extend its season. You could start the process cold in the bottom of the range oven, letting the fruit heat gradually with the oven, or you could put a large pan of cold water on top of the range, laying a piece of cardboard in the bottom of the pan to protect the jars from direct contact with the pan's hot base and to stop them rattling about too much. You put the fruit into the jars, brought the water to the boil, then put saucers on top of them, and simmered them gently. You pickled walnuts and onions, you made jams and jellies and wines from garden and hedgerow produce – and if you added sugar, there was the performance of preparing it: it was bought by the loaf rather than loose, so that you had to break it down and grind it yourself. And you bought milk preserved as butter and cheese, or did your own dairywork.

Your aim, like any haymaker, was to make the most of a food when it was in surplus by preserving what you could not immediately consume so that you had supplies to tide you through the leaner months. Some people in the '30s even had home canning equipment, though not many of them were true cottagers (it was easier to buy tinned goods at the shop). The rich had long had ice-houses in their grounds and insulated ice-chests, and by the '20s they also had massive refrigerators (the difference between an ice-chest and a refrigerator being that the former needs a supply of ice from elsewhere, often delivered by an itinerant iceman driving a cart lined with sawdust, while the latter makes its own ice). Cottagers continued to make do with naturally cold larders or the occasional touch of ingenuity like shoving snow into a chicken carcase or keeping liquids cool by dangling earthenware bottles in streams or down the well.

Perhaps they should have paid heed to the ever practical Cobbett, who had studied how the Virginians kept their fish and meat sweet even in their southern summers by simply making a raised bed three feet above ground level, of materials designed to shed the 'drippings' instantly, and standing out in the open and in the sun rather than buried expensively underground in the English country-house manner. A few poles and plenty of straw to insulate the ice blocks cut from winter lakes and the job was done, for a twentieth of the cost and, apparently, with far greater cooling efficiency than the elaborate English ice-houses. Anyway, as Cobbett said so scathingly, 'it is very hard to imagine, indeed, what any one should want ice *for*, in a country like this, except for clodpole boys to slide upon and to drown cockneys in skating time.' Cottagers, he said, were far more likely to want something to warm their blood than to cool it.

Talking of liquids, home brewing was widespread and most women could produce wines from almost any vegetable or fruit matter that came to hand. And how potent they were! I can well remember, as a teenager, tasting a neighbour's parsnip wine – and not much more than tasting – after which I found it happily difficult to follow the straightness of her garden path. Cider-making was another popular skill in apple-growing areas and I know of forgotten old cider-apple trees in unlikely places even now, their fruit small, bright and tart, their unpruned twigs all a-tangle as the gnarled old trees stand discreetly in the thicket of saplings betraying the overgrown garden of a vanished cottage in the woods. When those cottages still stood, it was the custom to do the rounds tasting each other's cider, weaving your way along the lanes and over the fields . . .

Which reminds me of George Dew's horse, sick with the colic. His master rubbed the animal's belly and dosed it with whisky, which effected a cure within three hours. Dew recalled his youth (he was born in 1846) when granny's family medicines included Calomel, Blue Pill, Antibilious Pills, Turkey Rhubarb and Grey Powder, whatever all those were. 'They had pretty nearly ruined all our constitutions,' complained Dew; indeed his sister, he said, was killed by too strong a dose of Calomel.

WATER

Being in a valley well sprinkled with large ponds and streams, my own village never lacked for water. There are several perpetual springs in the protective, tree-clad hangers that embrace this place and the valley itself was known for its high water table. Most of the scattered cottages and farms had their own wells if spring water was not close at hand, while within living memory rams pumped water up to some of the larger estates. That was how it was all over the country then.

Water has been a priority resource since time began and this country's early settlers naturally chose sites where water was readily available. That was fine while the ratio of people to land was reasonable: they drew their water from springs, ponds and streams or, where its presence was less obvious, they dug deep into the water table and sunk wells.

Victorian cottagers were accustomed to drawing water manually and carrying it into the house in pails for the family's every need. Shallow wells could be reached easily enough by letting your pail down on a pole with a spring-hook; deeper wells needed a winch so that a rope or chain could be wound up when the attached pail had taken its fill. There is, as those who have tried it will know, quite an art in sinking a wooden pail so that it can catch water – and the pails were always wooden (usually oak or elm), made by the same coopers who produced ale casks, until galvanized buckets began to find their way into country wells late in the Victorian period. The proper well bucket was a long one of wooden staves banded with steel, with a handle for the hook of the well rope.

Wellheads varied considerably. They might be nothing more than a few simple boards but were often good-looking, long-lasting examples of fine masonry or brickwork, with big, heavy wooden lids which kept out unwanted objects – including children. Many a mother fretted in case one of her offspring should tumble into a deep well and drown, which some did. Children also went down wells deliberately: Mavis Budd remembers in the 1920s taking her turn to help her father fix the workings of the pump, halfway down their very deep well. The pump was like a living animal – it had its good days and bad, and you could sense when its mood was deteriorating by tiny variations in its response as you worked the handle. It was rather like knowing how your car usually sounds and recognizing almost imperceptible new rattles and clunks as a sign of trouble. And, like a car, the pump tended to freeze up in winter so that its pipes had to be thawed

Woman and child by an unusually tidy well.

59

with the help of boiling water. Then everybody filled up every container they could find before it froze up again.

When the pump failed, the Budd children would have to traipse across the meadow to the nearest neighbour and carry back slurping buckets of water. Meanwhile father took one child with him into the endless black shaft to hold a light and hand him the right tools. They descended by ladder to a depth of about sixty feet, where there was a narrow, slippery wooden staging, dangerously rotten in places. All the way down they had tested the air with the help of a lighted candle, just like miners. Mavis dreaded falling through the staging into the water far below and her relief was huge when the mechanism was fixed and they could climb back up into the sunshine.

The family also caught as much rainwater as they could in waterbutts, and many a cottager used this stored water for washing, drinking and making tea. Some, living in high areas where water was a problem, had a more sophisticated system of storing rainwater in underground tanks which were supposed to hold enough water to last through a dry summer. The best of such systems incorporated a rainwater separator to divert the dirty first part of the flow of rainwater running off the cottage roof and gutters so that it did not contaminate the tank water. In theory, the larger the volume of the stored water, the smaller its proportion of surface to bulk and therefore the less its likelihood of being attacked by dirt and bacteria; in addition, bacterial activity was gradually reduced to the point of cessation if the water was stored in complete darkness. But underground storage tanks were a luxury unknown to most cottagers until perhaps the 1920s and 1930s, when the danger of polluted water sources was better appreciated. Where water was not readily available, many continued to rely on the old wooden waterbutt outside the back door, gathering rainwater from the roof. The average cottage roof would only harvest enough water for the traditional methods of cooking, drinking, laundry and, with luck, enough left over for one bath a week at the most. That was hardly adequate in volume for the rapidly improving standards of the 20th century.

Nor was it good enough in purity. The butt invariably collected and steeped algae, insects and other debris to add to the flavour but then, so did the well. Writing in the late 1930s, Frederick Smith and Barbara Wilcox described finding a decomposing mouse in a cottage well; a generation later, I found similar corpses in the well of a cottage which had been occupied by a blind man. Many a rat met a watery grave too, but cottagers seemed to develop an immunity to the effects of pollution in their own water supplies and claimed enviable purity for wells which were probably being infiltrated with kitchen sink water, general household rubbish, sewage and farmyard slurry. Wells also had a habit of drying up in a long summer . . .

Each cottage had its own well unless it was one of a close group of buildings – in a village, perhaps, or on an estate – when there would be a communal well, as often as not on the village green where everybody could meet for a good gossip on the pretext of drawing water. In some areas there were frequent wayside wells and water-troughs; in the south-west of the country there were road-runnels or 'pot-water' for use in times of shortage.

In due course villagers and cottagers replaced their well winches with the more sophisticated lever of the parish or backyard pump, its handle preferably of wood to give a kinder grip than iron on a frosty morning. The common pump had a lead pipe and was clad in some regions with elm weather-boarding, or might be a more ornate affair of iron. By the early 1920s, pumps were giving way to stand-pipes and new cottages began to have their own indoor water supplies.

The cottager's pump was as close to the scullery door as possible and even, eventually, just inside it – perhaps, oh joy, right over the shallow sink. The scullery sink was not necessarily waterproof itself; it was usually of wood, set on a brick plinth, though sometimes it was stone. It was used as a holder for a portable bowl – typically an earthenware redpan – and merely acted as a splash-catcher and stand, so that it required no drain hole itself: water was held in the portable bowl, which was handfilled and, after use, was tipped out into the garden. More often than not, the actual sink managed to attract hordes of woodlice and every other slug in the garden, with the occasional toad for good measure.

Some sinks were of shallow earthenware and later of galvanized iron; later in the Victorian period a few were of enamelled porcelain or glazed fireclay and became deeper, with drain-holes and plugs and some method of piping waste water out into a bucket or, eventually, down the drain. Some still preferred wooden sinks, perhaps lined with lead. Between the two world wars enamelled and glazed sinks became cheaper and much more common in cottages, usually with a wooden draining-board alongside.

WASHING

The redpan in the sink might be used on laundry day – a major occasion in the weekly calendar, which involved a great deal of hard work. Central to the whole operation was the copper, a huge container in which water was heated for washing. The copper (so called because it was usually made of that metal, though some were of iron) had a spherical rather than flat base and was set into its own brick plinth in the scullery. It was far from portable – so heavy that it needed two or even three people to take its weight. Underneath it had its own little fire in a tiny, square fireplace perhaps a foot or two square with its own little chimney. The fuel was usually bavins – bundles of twiggy brash which were also used to fire baking-ovens.

A washing copper, offered in sizes from 6 to 200 gallons, priced from 9 shillings to £15.

On laundry day you filled the copper with water and set it to boil up, filling the whole cottage with steam, especially in the many places which had no separate scullery and had to boil up in the kitchen/living-room. Then you lined up your redpans. Into one you put white sheets and pillowcases (one or two at a time); in another you put filthy working clothes for a good soak in soapy water – overalls and socks and trousers, coats and jumpers. There seemed to be so much more dirt around from landwork and gardening. Shirts and coloured clothes went into a third pan, and undies in a fourth. The men filled two pans with pure cold water, one with a blue-bag for whites, and the woman rubbed and rubbed in the hot soapy water, using her knuckles and a scrubbing brush on the dirtiest things as they were spread out on a corrugated washboard. Some used a dolly – a stout stick with a handlebar on the top and what looked like several stumpy stool legs at the bottom which were bashed against the clothes to loosen the dirt in hot water.

All the pans had to be filled with water by hand, using a pitcher to take hot water from the copper, and emptied by hand afterwards. By the end of the day, the copper was beautifully clean and shiny and it could be covered with its heavy wood top (very like a well cover, with a handle) to keep it clean for the rest of the week.

Then came the business of drying it all. Those who earned extra money by taking in washing would probably invest in a mangle but most cottagers simply wrung out what they could by hand and hung everything out in the garden over a hempen cord (which had to be taken down for the rest of the week to protect it from the rain, which tended to shrink it) or, by 1900, over a galvanized wire (whose coating often cracked and let rust stain the clothes), held in place by gypsy-made cleft wooden pegs banded with tin. Sheets might be draped over the hedges or hung from nails on the wall. In winter or wet weather, a line would be put up in the kitchen or scullery and wooden clothes-horses set around the fire or range, which was then banked up at night with coal dust to keep it going for what might be as long as a week of clothes-drying in winter, just in time to start all over again next laundry day. Oh, the smell of all those dank clothes hanging about the place – and they took up so much space! Cottage rooms, of course, were never high enough to accommodate those wooden drying racks suspended on pulleys near the ceiling.

Then there was the ironing, using flat-irons of different sizes – heavy ones for thick things and lighter ones for more delicate fabrics, and curling-irons for lacy edges. The irons were hung on a metal hook in front of the grate to heat, then you spread out an old blanket or sheet on the big wooden kitchen table and ironed there, resting the flat-iron on a pretty brass or iron stand to avoid burning the table.

What a performance! No wonder some women found such a ready market when they specialized in village or estate laundrywork. In my own village one such one-woman business continued to thrive until Mrs Lewis decided she was too old to bother in the 1950s, when her equipment became one of the first acquisitions of the new Museum of English Rural Life (MERL) on the campus of Reading University. Photographs of Mrs Lewis at work then make you appreciate why she decided to retire – the only wonder was that

Mrs Lewis in Laundry Cottage with her huge box mangle, early 1950s. She was a great favourite with local children, who dropped in for a chat when walking home from the village school.

this tiny woman had managed to wield her hefty equipment for fifty years. Even in 1953 she still used wooden sinks in the timber lean-to extension against her cottage, filling them with pipe-fed spring water (which today preserves her memory by insistently bubbling up in the lane outside her old cottage); in her own scullery she heated the water in several old-fashioned coppers built into their solid brick supports and filled with the help of a hose. What really caught MERL's eye, though, was Mrs Lewis's box-mangle in her hall. It was seven feet long; its hand-cranked wheel was as tall as she was, and it was encased in huge, heavy timbers, all weighed down with stones from broken 18th-century marble chimney-pieces.

The timber extension also housed an ordinary combustion stove, with a central chimney, where Mrs Lewis heated her thirty flat-irons, in brackets which each held nine. There was a long ironing counter in there, too, where she had dealt with the big house's laundry for so many years. At the time of her retirement she was taking in village laundry and charging a tanner for a shirt, four pence for a sheet, a shilling for a pair of flannel trousers and a penny a pair for socks. And she earned every farthing of it!

The first British washing-machine had been patented way back in 1691, incidentally, but it was another century and a half before the Americans began to develop the idea more seriously. By the mid 1920s machines were widely advertised in magazines aimed at middle-class women but they were way beyond a cottager's means – and anyway they needed piped water and plumbing, something few cottages could boast.

The scullery copper was also used for heating the cottage's bath water. Saturday night was the family bath night and the two-handled tin bath would be taken down from its nail in the scullery and set on the living-room floor in front of the fire or range. The men would discreetly take themselves into the scullery and read the paper and chat, giving the women and girls some privacy for their bath.

Bath night was a major event involving a great deal of work. Wood had to be chopped up and brought in to get the copper fire going; water had to be carried from the well or pump in endless bucketfuls and then slowly heated up in the copper, the fire being constantly tended in the meantime. Then the hot water from the copper was collected in jugs and small pails for transferring to the tin bath, and in you climbed, snugly surrounded by towels draped on clothes-horses to warm them by the fire and to protect you from draughts. A kettle was kept going on the fire so that the bath could be topped up as necessary. It was children first, in succession, then into their nightwear and straight to bed. The parents were the last in line and then came the business of emptying the bath, using a short-handled dipper to fill the pails rather than bailing out with the pails and pitchers which would then have dripped water all over the cottage as they were carried out to be emptied in the garden. Finally the floor splashes were wiped up, the towels draped to dry, the bath flannels squeezed out and suspended on a line over the range, and the bath itself was wiped dry and hung back on its nail until next week. The copper sat waiting for laundry day or for the winemaking session in which its belly played a central role (it might also be used as a boiling receptacle for Christmas puddings).

SANITATION

Water, oh water, the source of life and all too often the source of death as well. Some had the convenience of a stream at the bottom of the garden and I lived for a while in a tiny terraced Devon cottage at the damp head of an estuary, where the stream was quite literally outside the back door. You stepped out onto a yard-wide raised terrace which was all that separated the cottage wall from the water below, and usually the terrace was blanketed with sunbathing ducks.

That same cottage highlighted one of the major disadvantages – indeed dangers – of using stream water. At one end of the terrace, back to back with its neighbour, was the old privy which (you guessed it!) drained straight into the stream.

Streams did at least have a good enough natural flow in most seasons to carry away most of the effluent (bad luck on those who lived downstream). The problem could be much worse in well-water villages that practised the old system of digging a loo-hole in the garden at random. (Isn't it strange, by the way, that this very basic business, performed frequently by every single member of the human race, is so often glossed over in descriptions of everyday life? Well, I think it is time that you knew more about this fundamental function in the days before mains water and flushing toilets.)

English cottagers had to live with the family's evacuations, so to speak, rather than moving on after finding relief. Imagine the problems. Imagine not being able to pull a handle and let your bodily waste vanish in a swirl of cleansing water, out of sight and out of mind. The most basic solution is to dig a hole, make use of it for a while and then cover it over again, and that is exactly what most cottagers did, more or less, until at least the latter part of the 19th century. In some parts, however, especially on land that was not naturally well drained and in areas where cottages were close together, there was a gradual accumulation of effluent until raw sewage was standing in stagnant pools around the buildings or seeping down the village street.

George Dew, a Relieving Officer for the Bicester Poor Law Union, whose many duties including acting as a local health inspector, described in his 1870s diaries several horrifying examples of rural 'sanitation'. He came to one cottage where eight members of the family were suffering from typhoid fever, a common enough problem at the period. Two of this large family had already died. He took a sample of their pump water, which 'appeared as if very slightly tinged with soap-suds, and on holding it up in the bottle before the sun there could be seen an immense quantity of filaments . . . but the chief feature belonging to the water was a greasy film which immediately settled upon its surface.' This was the family's drinking water – and there is little doubt that it was well and truly contaminated with sewage. Elsewhere he found privies so full that their contents were spilling over the seat, and he fought a long local campaign on behalf of a row of cottages hard by an open sewage ditch which ran virtually beside their back walls. All over the country other worthies were fighting similar battles on cottagers' behalf and during the latter part of the 19th century there was an increasing realization that such sewage was responsible for the waves of epidemics, especially cholera and typhoid fever. Something, decided the Victorians, must be *done*.

There was a campaign to make sure that cottages and farmhouses had better sanitation arrangements at a time when neither type of household had as much as a properly managed earth closet which, in principle, meant a pail into which dry earth was sprinkled every time it was used, and eventually the contents of the pail were spread about under the topsoil to fertilize the garden. A privy, in essence, is a wooden seat above an open cesspit, whether indoors or outdoors, which has to be emptied by hand at regular intervals, the scooped-out contents being tranferred to a suitable depository by one means or another.

Pail for an earth closet,
'Holds 12 charges.'

All this human effluent needed space, and just as housed livestock too crowded during the winter can build up an unmanageable amount of manure, so too can humans when they begin to live too close together for too long. The land cannot take it! It was even worse in the towns, of course, where it became so bad that the authorities introduced the 'night soil' system: people were supposed to have a privy in the backyard and to cover its contents with earth or ashes in the approved fashion so that the contents were neutralized; then the local authority collected this night soil from every privy, more or less routinely, and laboriously took the stuff away to get it out of town, often selling it to farmers as manure.

Country areas did not have or need a removal service – most people had so much more space and they simply continued to deal with their own waste with varying degrees of efficiency. The privy was just that, a 'private place of ease' (as it is defined in the *Oxford English Dictionary*). It was a place where the act could be more private because a shed, permanent or portable, covered the chosen site. Privacy was certainly valued by the women in particular; Emily Lawrence remembers that the latter were very discreet

Down the garden path to a dilapidated privy in Herefordshire.

about such matters, sneaking secretly down·the garden to the privy and never talking about such things in front of the men.

Very few cottages had space for an indoor privy, except perhaps in a lean-to. The outside privy was often under a yew tree, partly for added privacy and partly because the tree was said to deter the flies that were invariably attracted. You still had to dash down the length of the garden to visit this more private hole, whether it was in the middle of the night or the middle of a snowstorm when the urge overtook you, but at least it was relatively snug inside, with a wooden plank to sit on. There would be at least one square hole in the plank; some were two-seaters and some had an extra, smaller hole for a child so that mum could train it in the art of privy-using without the child falling down an adult-sized hole! The privy seat was scrubbed to whiteness every Saturday, when the toilet paper was replaced – sheets of newspaper cut into squares and threaded on a string or piled into a box on the plank. The privy walls might be decorated with calendar pictures – shops were overgenerous with free calendars, and pictures of Queen Victoria or paintings by Turner were carefully cut out to brighten not only the privy but also the scullery and the back of the doors.

So what went on under that plank? At first it was the familiar hole in the ground, with a homemade soakaway and a bucketful of ashes, or of earth which had been dried in the sun during the day, and this material would be sprinkled over the effluent to soak up some of it and to control the stench. In better privies the ash-bucket was kept in a little cupboard under the seat and the obvious next stage was to use a bucket as a receptacle instead of just a hole in the ground which had to be re-dug elsewhere at intervals. Some people had big, oval, galvanized pails known as lavatory buckets – they had to be big to accommodate any splashing. When the bucket was full with its mixture of effluent and ashes or earth, the man of the house had the task of digging a hole in the garden (as before!) and emptying the contents into it, then washing out the bucket with pump water. This hole was covered with a board and marked with a stick so that a good gardener would rotate this sensible use of organic material and gradually manure the whole of the vegetable patch.

A slightly unusual version in one of my valley's cottages was so close to the stream that they simply dug a ditch from the privy hole to the stream and flushed it out with a pailful of water when they remembered, which was hardly pleasant for their downstream neighbours. This was not back in the Dark Ages, mind you, but between the two world wars.

In due course cottagers were encouraged to use chemicals in their buckets – the Elsan touch – which turned solids into liquid but produced a vile smell and the bucket still had to be emptied.

Better privies were quite well built, with brick floors and boltable doors, but most were haphazard affairs and there is many a tale of doors that would

Moule's patent 'Pull-Up' earth closet, which 'throws one and a half pints of earth each time the closet is used.' Stand well back!

Jennings's 'Servants and Cottage' Victorian WC, with varnished pine seat. 'Hard Wood Birch Seat in place of Pine 7/6d extra.'

not shut or which suddenly flew open at inconvenient moments, and of chickens roosting and rats scurrying. It was said that children evacuated from the cities during the war frequently reverted to bedwetting in country cottages as they were so terrified of the journey down the garden path at night into the shadowy privy, guided only by a flickering candle in its draughty lantern (if that), which was inclined to extinguish itself suddenly and leave you trembling in the dark, at the mercy of every passing spook and vampire. In reality most cottagers kept chamberpots under the bed for night-time peeing (and only peeing) and the contents were usually thrown into the hedge in the morning. So that's why cottage boundary ditches are always happy homes for stinging nettles!

David Creaton, in his book *The Beasts of my Field*, knew all about privies. The family decided that they could not expect their visitors to 'take a deep breath as they headed across the backyard, deep enough to last them at least part of the way through a speedy session in the privy.' But, as he pointed out, an earth closet 'may pong a bit, but it never freezes up.' And it helped the adjacent quince tree to produce a huge crop of excellent fruit, too, until they decided to install an indoor flushing toilet and let the privy to Mrs P.P. – alias Mrs Puffy Pecker, an old hen who chose the abandoned privy seat as the ideal site for hatching a brood of chicks.

Mavis Budd, who lived in a village near to my own and who wrote a delightful book (*Dust to Dust*) about her childhood there in the 1920s, described their ancient privy 'built of sandstone, with the ruins of the original earth pit at the back'. It stood under a huge laurel tree at the top of the garden and her father had modernized it by putting in a wooden seat and a varnished front partition to hide the bucket. The privy's door had blown off in a storm long ago and was propped against the wall, half hidden by several years of ivy growth (father would get around to fixing the door . . . one day) so that anyone who sat in the privy was in full view of the cottage. Father minded not a bit: he would sit there of an early morning in summer with his trousers about his ankles, reading the old newspapers or singing hymns and rude ballads. The four children also liked to linger when the 'morning privy was warmed with sunshine. Birds hopped on the roof tiles, searching in the crevices for insects brought out by the warmth' while the child secretly (and illicitly) read the newspapers for their worldly gossip. Dappled sunlight, birds' nests in the rampant ivy, pretty yellow snails under the eaves – it was really quite a charming summerhouse. But the winter privy was very different: its walls, whitewashed every August bank holiday, would be stained with rain water, beetles hid in the papers, rats scuttled along a shelf under the eaves where father stored bottles of rat poison. The children hated the winter dash there through rain and wind over the slippery cinder path and absolutely refused to visit it alone after dark, going to extreme lengths to bribe a companion if the urge was overwhelming.

Every six months the Budd children earned tuppence by digging a large, deep hole at the bottom of the garden, right down to the hard layer of yellow sandstone, into which the contents of the privy bucket were emptied at weekly intervals. Father was not a gardener by inclination and did not bother to recycle the stuff as manure on the vegetable patch.

It was a red-letter day, as you can imagine, when mains water at last came to the post-war cottagers. In some places, major land-owners had built their own reservoirs (originally for fire-fighting) and piped the water to their estate cottages, but these were rare. Proper mains water meant taps instead of pumps and wells, and the possibility of indoor WCs instead of privies. Water closets had in fact been invented long ago – a 1596 prototype, and the first patents in the 1770s, when Alexander Cummings introduced his Bond Street valve-closet, a vigorous flusher which remained popular in some upper-class homes for a century of gradual refinement. By 1870 Twyfords were making wash-out closets and by the 1890s someone had designed the wash-down pan shape still used today. But for a long time such utilities remained luxuries enjoyed only by the better off, and certainly not cottagers. Sydney Jones, writing in the 1930s, told of a new council house's mahogany WC seat being removed by the occupant to make a fine frame for grandad's photo, and of an old villager who, being asked if she liked her new plumbed bath, replied with feeling, 'Thank God, sir, I has never had occasion to use it!'

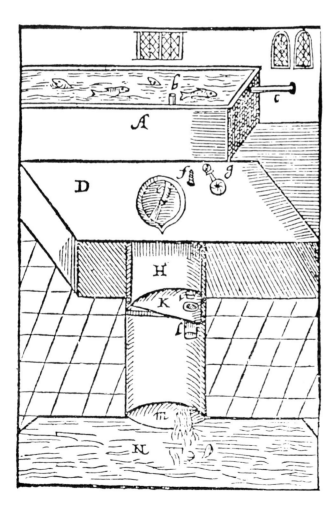

Early design for a water-closet by Sir John Harrington.
(*Metamorphosis of Ajax*, 1596).

71

Mains water was not necessarily marvellous – it depended on which water source fed the mains, and all too often in the 19th century it was the local river-cum-sewer. But matters gradually improved.

Indoor plumbing was a new idea for cottagers used to carrying water to where it was needed and carrying it away again when it was dirty. Plumbing meant that you simply turned a tap to get fresh, cold water from the mains and pulled out a plug or yanked a WC chain to get rid of it into your cesspit. Cesspits were simple but reasonably efficient: they were basically just very large holes in the ground and they had to be emptied periodically, a job eventually taken over by local councils. In the early 1940s new country dwellers were being advised that a cesspool should be of a sufficient size to take a month's waste water, allowing a thousand gallons per head. Much better was the septic tank, which only rarely needed emptying, if at all. In principle a septic tank is a series of brick or concrete underground chambers and pipes: domestic waste drains into the first tank and is decomposed by anaerobic bacteria (which flourish only in the absence of oxygen) while solids and fats collect on the surface for decomposition by other bacteria. Well below this layer of scum is a pipe outlet which takes the partially decomposed liquid to a second tank for further anaerobic decomposition until a liquid emerges into a series of shallow, spreading, horizontal drains just below ground surface where aerobic bacteria (taking oxygen from the covering shallow layer of porous soil) complete the purification process so that virtually clean water is left to soak away or drain into the nearest watercourse.

Many a cottage still has its cesspool or septic tank system in the garden today and many a village was given a communal sewage works. These systems operated perfectly well in most cases, within their limited capacity – and that was the problem. With mains water came a huge increase in the use of flushing toilets and regular baths, both of which not only took a high volume of water from the mains (where available) but also discharged a high volume of waste water into the local sewage systems, causing some very unpleasant flooding, especially on areas of heavy clay. In theory, sewage systems were supposed to be sited at least fifty feet from any dwelling place or public or trade building and not less than sixty feet from any source of water intended for drinking or domestic use such as wells, springs and streams; in practice this often proved impossible in congested villages. That was how it was in 1940, when an author describing country living suggested that earth closets and chemical closets, though much despised, were actually less trouble than many water-flushed sewage systems and were fully approved by the sanitary authorities of the time.

Many cottagers installed their first plumbed-in baths and WCs in the 1950s or later, when mains water at last reached them. They usually put them in a lean-to, perhaps an old workshed or pighouse, or converted the old scullery downstairs with its familiar cold, damp and spiders. Quite often such a room's floor was solid and was below the outside ground level, which added to the dampness and cold, and thus many remain even now.

Plumbing brought you more than cold water, of course: for the first time in their lives cottagers were able to have hot water on tap as well, if the black range or open fire was fitted with a back boiler and a few pipes. Most homes had back boilers by the kitchen chimney or livingroom fire-place by the '30s and '40s. Superior houses had had hot water on tap since the 1850s but even average houses did not get mains water until the early 20th century, along with electricity, though cottagers, as usual, had to wait another generation for such luxuries.

There had been attempts to bring mains drainage to rural areas as early as the 1870s but they were disastrous; the systems were so badly designed and built that local water supplies were seriously polluted and everyone was put off the whole idea of public sewage systems. However, mains drainage gradually came to the villages, even if it has still not reached outlying hamlets and scattered cottages and farms. In most cases it came in time to cope with the even greater volume of waste water created in recent years by the use of washing machines and dishwashers – imagine, if you will, how the cottager of old would have been overwhelmed by the volume of water such machines now use, how many hand-carried bucketfuls . . . Country cottagers today, mind you, have little choice than to be 'green': our garden cesspools and septic tanks become inoperable if we use detergents and bleaches, which kill off all those helpful bacteria. The Greens would do well to offer town-dwellers three-month country cottage relocations (preferably in winter) so that people could experience at first hand just how their own effluent can cause them problems when it is not magically taken away by mains drainage to cause problems somewhere else!

RUBBISH

The same is true of rubbish, and I challenge any family in the land to put themselves into the following alarming scenario: every bit of waste, be it effluent or dustbin rubbish, generated by your family must be disposed of by you within your own curtilage. That is how it was for cottagers and that, combined with varying degrees of poverty, made quite sure that they wasted very little indeed. They patched and mended, they recycled, they squeezed every last breath of life out of their material goods before reluctantly discarding them. Economy was the cottager's creed.

Rubbish had to be disposed of at home. There were three complementary methods: composting, burning and burial, all of which took place in the garden or nearby wasteland. That is to say, cottagers and villagers lived with the consequence of disposal as it was on their very doorstep rather than on someone else's miles away. There was no anonymity about cottage rubbish. Many city dwellers had the luxury of galvanized dustbins being emptied at irregular intervals by the council in the 1930s, but dustbin collection in rural areas was, as usual, a later development and even now some of us have only fortnightly collections, for which we might have to cart our own bins down long, rough tracks to the lane because the new refuse lorries, in the interests of 'economy', are too big to squeeze between the hedgerows.

Two garden bonfires burned almost incessantly in the old cottage gardens – a woman's fire on which she boiled up pig swill and chicken feed, and a man's on which rubbish was ultimately burned. Organic matter was added to the swill or composted for use on the garden in time-honoured fashion. Tins and jars were buried along the hedges, or made into garden banks and rockeries, or even carefully buried end-up to form pathways (much ingenuity was needed to make paths passable in muddy weather), and many a brick path was edged with up-turned paste jars and jam jars. Bottles might be made into walls, bonded with cement, and I know of a little cottage near Reading whose front wall was embedded with green bottles, their whirly bases facing outwards in imitation of old-fashioned 'bottle glass', creating an intriguing effect. They probably provided quite good insulation, too.

Pots and pans were mended endlessly and when they became really beyond repair they were used as patching material for other vessels. Broken crockery, as all gardeners know, tended to be thrown into the vegetable patch at random or added to ashes for the paths or buried with the jars and old batteries and endless bits of unidentifiable, rusty old iron bits and pieces. There was, of course, no plastic or polythene to deal with and very little packaging until after the Great War; before then, most goods were sold loose or in reusable cotton bags and sacking, and many people took their own receptacles to the village shop to fill them up with basic items like sugar, tea and flour.

CLEANING

Cleaning was a constant labour, especially if you had open fires and men who worked on the land or in other jobs that inevitably brought a fair amount of dirt home with them. I can remember, in my village school domestic science class in the 1950s, learning the weekly rigmarole of scrubbing down the wooden tables to keep them white – vicious on the knuckles.

Cleaning materials included all sorts of homemade polishes, soaps and other aids like lime-and-sand for scouring tables, pieces of the horsetail plant for scouring metal, whiting for hearths and doorsteps, and cuttlefish bone as an abrasive. Ash from wood fires was steeped in a barrel of soft water to be turned into washing lye; hen manure mixed with urine could bleach linen, though most preferred to let sunlight do the job instead!

By the turn of the century, village stores were already stocking mass-produced cleaning aids and by the '20s the village carrier's cart was bringing branded goods to the cottage door. Now that reading was almost a universal skill, with the great improvements in education, companies were realizing the advantages of advertising goods that had become nationally available – *packaged* goods at that, like Cherry Blossom boot polish, Lux soap flakes, Bronco toilet paper, Robin starch, Sunlight Soap and many more. The recipes for homemade aids were quickly being forgotten, though some of the favourite raw materials like washing soda would persist for many years yet.

In the early years of the 20th century cottagers often still used the traditional birch besoms and heather brooms made by local broomsquires (or broomsquarers) and costing three shillings and sixpence a dozen for birch or half-a-crown a dozen for heather in 1900. The hearth was swept with a goose-wing, its feathers gradually singed away by hot soot and ashes, but the quills could still make a good job of brushing such matter out of the fireplace's many nooks and crannies and a goose-wing could be made to last for a year, until another goose was eaten at Christmas. By the 1880s, however, Ewbank's hand-propelled carpet-sweeper was being used in better houses – but of course cottagers had no carpets! An electrically driven vacuum cleaner, based on a pillowcase and a broomstick, was created in Ohio in 1908 and Hoovers were being sold on tick, door to door, in Europe just before the Great War – but cottagers had no electricity, and when electricity did arrive in the '40s and '50s many of them were too terrified to use it anyway.

THE GREAT OUTDOORS

WILDLIFE

MAVIS BUDD'S cottage was a new one, two up and two down with a tin-roofed lean-to kitchen, and it was tacked on to a very old cottage inhabited by her grandparents. It is the latter cottage that she brings to life so vividly in her 1920s memoirs. It had a pump; it had leaves in its gutters, moss everywhere, roses around the door and moonlight in all the rooms. Crowds of birds lived in its roof, nesting and roosting and arguing there and littering the back kitchen with feathers, droppings, nesting materials and dead fledglings. The big black kitchen chimney smoked and there were no drains (grandfather, a builder by trade, had deliberately blocked them all by way of 'improvement'). There were mice in the walls and sometimes rats. There were many cats which slept their lives away by the fire or out in the sunshine – the rats and the cats seemed to be oblivious to each other.

The cottage, said to be over four hundred years old, was 'riddled with cracks and holes and scars which were steadily enlarged by birds, mice and insects . . . There were beetles, the rich blue of sapphires, quick moving, furtive and shy. They lived beneath the mats and in the dark undisturbed corners. And of course there were quantities of spiders. In fact there were so many it was impossible to get rid of them. The largest ones, when swept out, just turned around and came in again. Fortunately no one in the cottage really objected to them. Granny would have been afraid of them, but then she was far too blind to notice.'

Autumn leaves filtered into the rooms and hid in corners, ready to swirl in sudden whirlpools at the whim of every passing draught. Bindweed found its way everywhere, wreathing in under unused doors and through rotted woodwork, coiling around table legs; forlorn wisps of light-starved grass grew where the damp walls met the damp floor; climbing plants poked their pale heads through cracks in the mortar; moss decorated the windowsills; algae and fungi revelled in the wall-damp; tiny weeds sprouted between the floor bricks and, every now and then, a mole would heave up its earth-heap in the middle of the brick-floored main room. Starlings dislodged the plaster from its battens; bats flew in through holes in the roof and the children dealt with that problem by lighting candles – the bats, like the moths, flew to the light, became confused, bumped into the wall and knocked themselves out so that they could be picked up gently and released outside.

There were woodlice, ants and beetles all over the cottage, including vicious looking devil's coach-horses and cockroaches. Access to the cottage was so easy for them – all the downstairs rooms, with their brick floors, had holes in the walls so that water could be swept out after the floors had been washed.

Jefferies noted that so many cottages and farmhouses left their outside doors open as a matter of course (often to rid the room of the smoke that belched from the huge open-chimney fireplace) that frogs, toads and the occasional snake wandered in quite freely and were accepted as part of everyday indoor life. My own cottage garden today, in a valley well stocked with ponds, is home to many amphibians. When I returned home in a downpour one summer night and opened my back door in a hurry, a tiny toadlet scampered indoors with me and adamantly refused to go out again.

Cottages have always been wildlife havens! I remember another of my cottage homes where black beetles used to scurry harmlessly across the floors every evening, so familiar that they almost became pets. Luckily they were not destructive, but many a cottage suffered from the cockroaches that so often infested village bakehouses, covering entire walls and ceilings in the dark of the night. These loved sweet things and also had a passion for beer. They could be trapped in jamjars, baited with stale beer and banana, with a cardboard ramp up to a cardboard lid with a hole in its middle containing a paper cone.

In the 1940s, the cottage 'pests' were much the same as they had always been and so were the steps taken against them by those who bothered. Rats? Protect your food supplies – put wire screens over the larder window and invest in a metal food-safe. Incinerate food scraps or boil them up for the chickens rather than burying them on the compost heap. Call in a rat-catcher or find a good strain of rat-catching cat, terrier or ferret. In the '40s the Ministry of Agriculture was recommending a rat poison of equal parts of barium carbonate powder, grated cheese or pounded kipper, fine oatmeal and melted dripping, all mixed into a paste and set as bait wrapped in screws of tissue paper; I could tell you of more unpleasant ones involving sawdust and cement but I would rather not. Mousetraps (other than cats) were homemade and often ingenious, if brutal – like the 'deadfall' types which basically dropped a very heavy wooden block on their victims.

Fleas often infested old cottages, hiding in woodwork and decayed plaster and thatch, sometimes to such a degree that they set the seal on the numerous cottage demolition orders that followed a surge of concern for rural dwellings between the wars. Sometimes the family pig attracted fleas in spring and these transferred quite happily to human hosts, as did those that usually fed on cats, dogs, rats or poultry. George Dew, writing in the 1870s, had visited the cottage of an elderly couple where 'fleas were hopping about the floor in numbers, & they had lice (light horsemen as some ludicrously call them) also.' Bed bugs, however, seem to have been less of a problem in the country than in the cities and indeed evacuee children were often blamed for introducing them.

A major country problem was flies, especially in the vicinity of farm livestock – those biting horseflies (you could soothe the wound with witch hazel) and the omnipresent bluebottles which laid their eggs in fresh manure and were either swatted or caught on sticky paper strips, dangling in curls from the middle of the room. It was believed that flies would be deterred from entering a room or cowshed if its interior walls were painted blue.

Mosquitoes made themselves at home on stagnant ponds and cottagers would spray the pond with kerosene or put saucers containing oil of lavender or oil of citronella on their windowsills at night to deter adult mosquitoes from entering. Jefferies described 45-year-old John Smith's hovel in Wiltshire in the 1870s – just two downstairs rooms (one so small he could reach across it), rain coming through the thin thatch, a floor of hard mud, and one of the wattle-and-daub shanty walls rising up from the edge of a large stagnant pond into which all the cottage's sewage and the land's surface water drained. At night, because of the pond, 'there was almost always a thick damp mist, which crept in through the crevices of the rotten walls, and froze the blood in the sleepers' veins. Sometimes a flood came down, and the pond rose and washed away the cabbages from the garden . . .' The mosquitoes must have relished such a pond as an ideal breeding place.

There were more welcome visitors, like the chirruping fireside cricket (in spite of its unfortunate habit of devouring seedlings), and countless cottagers kept a wild bird or two in a small wicker cage hung in the front porch – songbirds like thrushes, blackbirds, nightingales and linnets, or a corvid which could be taught mimicry like a parrot. Sometimes the cage was brought indoors and hung from a nail driven into a ceiling joist, perhaps joining all those other items that dangled from such nails, such as baskets, tools, herbs, lanterns, onions, hams and empty beehives.

BACKYARD BEASTS

Bees were kept by many a cottager, usually in traditional skeps made from straw ropes wound like a basket and bound with thinly shaved hazel rods or withies, and perhaps roofed with a broken redpan or more carefully protected in a special alcove or 'bee bole' in the garden wall. A swarm of bees could be claimed by the person on whose property it happened to settle – and in May (when swarming usually began) the sound of ploughshares being beaten with heavy old door-keys advertised the action of someone trying to attract a swarm in midflight so that they could quickly transfer it to the spare hive kept in readiness on the nail in the back kitchen.

Cottager's straw beehives protected with sacking and the two halves of a broken redpan.

Chickens, naturally, were common in cottage gardens; geese grazed on the village green and some kept a turkey or two in a run for Christmas. Others specialized in duck-rearing; a few might keep a goat or two, and the more fortunate a house cow, but many more would keep a couple of pigs and relied on their meat. They would buy a couple of young weaners (paying the customary shilling down on the bargain as a binding deposit) and feed them on household scraps and pigmeal until they were fit for slaughter. The scraps included peelings (but never of onions), potato chats and fallen apples, all boiled up in the scullery copper or in a big iron pot set on a piece of iron over the permanent garden bonfire, then mixed with pigmeal to make a mash. The meal was bought from the village shop or a local farm. The weaners grew fatter and fatter, and the bigger they grew the more they ate so that the time came when the cottager could no longer afford to buy pigmeal and so the dirty deed must be done. Until that moment, the family pig had also been a family pet and a source of pride to be shown off to neighbours and scratched by friends and talked to by everybody.

Then a local butcher or travelling pig-sticker would be summoned on the pig's last day. Most pigs were killed at home and a great occasion was made of the event. The killer – often the postman or someone else who had made pig-killing his sideline – would do the actual deed but with the family's help and a great deal of heart-rending squealing from the pig. The blood from its cut throat would be carefully collected for black puddings and the whole family would help with scalding the newly dead pig in boiling water before laying its body on a low oak bench or hog-form to scrape off all its hairs. The carcase would be suspended from a hind leg roped to a beam, waiting for the butcher to return a few days later and chop it into manageable hunks.

Cobbett gave very detailed pig-keeping instructions in his *Cottage Economy* (1823), recommending that the animals be a year old before being killed. 'This age is required in order to insure the greatest quantity of meat from a given quantity of food,' he said, advising that 'if he can walk two hundred yards, he is not well-fatted.' Modern nutritionists might shudder but Cobbett went on to say: 'Lean bacon is the most wasteful thing that any family can use. In short, it is uneatable, except for drunkards, who want something to stimulate their sickly appetite. The man who cannot live on *solid fat* bacon, well fed and well cured, wants the sweet sauce of labour, or is fit for the hospital.' He said that the best time for the kill was about Christmas, in coldish weather, and that 'to kill a hog nicely is so much of a profession, that it is better to pay a shilling for having it done, than to stab and hack and tear the carcass about.' Nonetheless, he gave details on slaughtering and butchering and also on salting and smoking bacon and ham, claiming that properly cured bacon could last a year, or even two or three, if protected from maggots by being stored in deep layers of woodfire ashes. Yum yum. Hmm.

COTTAGE GARDENS

The English cottage garden: what an idyllic image! During the 19th century Mrs Allingham captured the idyll in her watercolours but she was often guilty of considerable artistic licence, which the cynic might immediately suspect from the title of her book, *Happy England*.

There was a time, from the 16th century onwards, when no new cottage could be built unless it had at least four acres of ground for a garden and to support home livestock. The enclosures movement not only deprived cottagers of much commonland grazing but also shrank many of their gardens to half an acre or less – and in some cases *much* less. Many a cottager was allowed no more than a small back yard and perhaps a tiny patch of ground between the front and the lane. For the cottager, a reasonable-size garden was a practical environment that allowed a high degree of self-sufficiency. It was a place for growing vegetables and rearing small livestock; it was also the site of the wood pile, the coal shed, the lean-to workshop and the tool shed, the well or pump and the privy, and was a general rubbish tip for discarded household items, slops, kitchen waste and other manure.

The real cottage garden was more likely to be a cinder-pathed utility patch than a glorious riot of summer colour and scent. Grass, if there was any, was strictly for grazing livestock – the idea of a 'lawn' was laughable when the only other way of cutting it was with the aid of a scythe or sickle.

Loudon, already mentioned (see p. 37) as giving advice better suited to the weekender's *cottage orné* than to the real cottager, was also less than practical in his cottage gardening, though he was a nurseryman by profession. As co-author of the *Complete Gardener* in the early years of the 18th century, he did not even mention that cottage staple, the potato. Another popular horticultural author of the time, one Bradley, wrote of potatoes that 'they are of less note than horse-radish, scorzonera, beets, and

Cottage pigs at the bottom of the garden.

skirret'. The contemporary Harrison, remarking that only the gentry ate bread made from wheat, wrote that cottagers, labourers and artisans were 'driven to content themselves with horse corne, beanes, peason, oats, tares and lentils': their bread, if any, was made from barley, rye or oats and he made no mention at all of potatoes. Baxter of Lewes, who published a huge tome grandly entitled *Baxter's Library of Agricultural and Horticultural Knowledge* in the early 1830s, noted that in his own boyhood in Wintringham, Lincolnshire, the older inhabitants had told him how they remembered 'fetching a basket of potatoes on Saturday afternoons from a neighbouring village as an extraordinary dainty, it never occurring for many years to these good people that the cultivation of this vegetable was within the sphere of their own ability.' He also reported that the local squire's wife in those days had been sent a pound of tea as a gift; flummoxed, she boiled it like spinach and served it on a plate with melted butter!

Potatoes had in fact been known in England since about 1586. For most of the 17th century they were treated as rare, exotic plants which provided the occasional treat for the wealthy – the accounts of James I's queen Ann, for example, recorded the price of this luxury as a shilling a pound. Although the Royal Society was keen to promote the potato and drew its virtues to the attention of Evelyn as early as 1663, he did not bother to write about it until the 1690s – and then he recommended putting those little green 'apples' occasionally produced by potato plants into a salad, clearly unaware that they are poisonous. Mortimer's *Gardener's Kalendar* for 1708 kindly explained that the potato (obviously still an oddity) was 'very near in nature of the Jerusalem artichoke, although not so good and wholesome, but that it may prove good for swine.' Artichokes had long been held in high esteem.

In France, the use of potatoes was violently opposed for two centuries or more, until Louis XV wore a bunch of potato blossom at court. In England, William Cobbett detested the very thought of potatoes in the cottage – they were as unwanted as tea. Tea, he declaimed, 'has no *useful strength* in it; that it contains nothing *nutricious*; that it besides being *good* for nothing, has *badness* in it, because it is well known to produce want of sleep in many cases, and in all cases, to shake and weaken the nerves. It is, in fact, a weaker kind of laudanum, which enlivens for the moment and deadens afterwards.' Home-brewed beer was a far better drink for the cottager, and also a great deal cheaper when tea was five bob a pound – and the business of tea-making was so time-consuming when you took into account making the fire, boiling the water, making and drinking the tea, washing up, sweeping the fireplace and so on, for which he allowed two hours!

Cobbett dismissed 'the modern custom of using *potatoes* to supply the place of *bread*'. He was greatly shocked that in the west of England in particular it had become the custom to allot to labourers a 'potatoe ground' in part payment of wages. 'This', he remonstrated, 'has a tendency to bring English labourers down to the state of the Irish, whose mode of living, as to food, is but one remove from that of the pig, and of the ill-fed pig too.' What was his objection? Well, for a start there were the 'slovenly and beastly habits engendered amongst the labouring classes by constantly lifting their principal food at once out of the earth to their mouths, by eating without the necessity of any implements other than the hands and the teeth, and by dispensing with every thing requiring skill in the preparation of the food and requiring cleanliness in its consumption or preservation.' Then there was the fact (surely a point in favour?) that an acre of land which could produce 32 bushels of wheat could instead produce 300 bushels of potatoes – but he claimed that once the water, the 'stringy substance' and the earth were removed from the potato crop there remained only a tenth of that weight in nutritious matter, and anyway wheat, once sown, looked after itself while potatoes needed constant cultivation. Wheat produced good straw as a by-product infinitely superior to potato haulm. And there was the huge labour of lifting and storing potatoes, and the risk of loss to frost. Then there was the cost of cooking, and here Cobbett went through a complicated argument which thoroughly fiddled the figures by claiming that you needed nine hundred boilings of the pot a year for daily potatoes to replace bread, whereas the latter took only 32 heatings of the oven to bake it. And there was the labour of peeling and scraping and washing, for at least the English did not eat potatoes in the Irish style, 'that is to say, scratch them out of the earth with their paws, toss them into a pot without washing, and when boiled, turn them out upon a dirty board, and then sit round that board, peel the skin and dirt from one at a time and eat the inside.'

Cobbett prejudiced? Perish the thought! He goes on for several more pages about 'leaving Ireland to her *lazy* root'.

Cobbett was writing in the early 1820s but during that century others appreciated the value of the potato. Baxter, citing one Mac Innes, said that of all the esculent roots the potato was 'undoubtedly the best entitled to our careful cultivation', whether for man or beast. Indeed he grew lyrical, describing it as 'one of the very first boons of Providence'. Said Baxter, in about 1830: 'When we consider it, either as smoking in solitary importance on the labourer's humble board, or as taking its customary place among the viands of the great, the potato is equally welcome.' He then listed a wide range of varieties with delightful names such as Fox's Seedling, Early Manly, Broughton Dwarf, Nonsuch, Red-nose Kidney, Bread-Fruit, Lancashire Pink-eye, Red Apple, Black Skinned, and the 'excellent varieties of party-coloured potatos in Scotland'.

Potato-growing needed more space than was available in many cottage gardens but those who could grow such a valuable vegetable did so. To preserve the lifted crop so that it lasted the winter, they often built clamps – either digging a deep hole for a pile of potatoes covered by a thick-walled makeshift hut of clay and straw, or simply piling the crop on the surface of the ground, surrounded by a deep trench, and covered thickly with straw under a jacket of trench spoil beaten down in layers to make a good, frostproof cover. In severe cold such a heap was further protected with a coating of steaming muck. And if the potatoes did get frosted, they were apparently none the worse for it as long as they were carefully thawed out in darkness; they rotted if thawed in daylight.

Potatoes offered more than food for the cottager and cottage livestock. The stalks produced a cottony flax, the roots could give sugar and spirits, the 'apples' vinegar. And you could even try to make soap from the tubers, or a bleach substitute. A more important use was in making starch, and the sieved refuse from starch-making possessed the property of cleansing woollen cloth without affecting its colour.

But some still regarded the potato with deep suspicion, claiming that after a hot, dry summer the tubers were poisonous and that if eaten as a staple diet they were a 'proximate cause' of typhus fever.

The closely related tomato faced similar prejudice, especially as it was known as the love-apple. To discourage its use as an aphrodisiac, the word was put about that it was a poisonous fruit and even in Baxter's time the love-apple was rare. The Victorians eventually gave it credibility but cottagers usually lacked the glasshouse facilities to grow their own tomatoes. Incidentally, I knew of a dedicated cowman in the 1970s, still living with his unmarried brother and sister and their aged parents in a very small farm cottage with only the most basic facilities (they still used an outside privy, for example), who was a passionate vegetable gardener. He and his 80-year-old father really did have green fingers and their patch was a joy to see, nourished by many years of cow manure (and no doubt privy manure), neatly laid out with rows of perfect vegetables. He grew for the pleasure of doing so and for the pleasure of giving away excess produce, of which there was a great deal. One day he made himself a greenhouse from hazel poles draped with old bits of clear polythene and here he grew tomatoes. He also experimented and grew aubergines and peppers. However, the latter perplexed the family in the kitchen. They carefully peeled them and were left with nothing to eat but air, seeds and the small core.

This good man always planted his potatoes on Easter Monday, regardless of whether it was early March or late April. Oh well, at least he avoided the Good Friday dilemma. If you lived in the Midlands, Good Friday was *the* day for potato planting; but if you lived in the south, that was the one day on which you must *not* set your tubers.

Roots were important cottage crops. Turnips were a great favourite: they could be put into stews and broths, or boiled and mashed, and their tops made useful spring greens. Carrots, gradually improved from the wild kind found on every verge, were essential; parsnips, too, especially in the old days of Catholicism when they were served with salted fish in Lent. Some traditionally used caraway roots instead of parsnips. Many grew beet – white beet for greens, red for beetroot – and radishes, whose seed pods could be pickled like capers. Horseradish was grown if there was some marshy ground, and it was not only grated into a sauce but also formed the basis of a grease used on sprained or rheumatic joints. Every sort of onion found a place in the cottage garden, including spring onions, shallots, chives and leeks.

Cabbage was perhaps the most important and best-loved vegetable of all and was the essential accompaniment for meals based on potatoes and pigmeat; Baxter listed countless varieties for every season and situation, including the amazing cow cabbage, grown as food for cattle but also for its massive, tough stems which were used as walking sticks and as supports for roof thatch and other building purposes. Many grew kale, broccoli and cauliflowers, and in due course Brussels sprouts (not common until later in the 19th century). Spinach was very popular – with care there could be a fresh supply almost all year round, and the same was true for cress: in winter people really craved their greens. Chicory was also grown, largely as food for the pig or cow, but also to grind the roots as mock coffee (dandelion roots and acorns served the same purpose). Some grew celery and celeriac; many used alexanders as a celery substitute; and many grew lettuce for their salads.

Then there were the pods – peas a great favourite, broad beans as a staple food (especially the cottage 'Long-pod') and runner beans for their flowers as much as their pods. Baxter pointed out that these climbing beans twisted up their rods in the opposite direction to the sun's movement, unlike native climbers, because, he said, they came from South America.

Borage was grown partly as food (you could cook the roots and boil the young shoots), partly for its pretty flowers that endeared it to bee-keepers, and partly as a herb. Bees were attracted to the blossom of buckwheat, a useful plant in that its seed could be fed to the cottage pig and the chickens. Hemp was still widely grown in the early 19th century: its seeds apparently served to increase a hen's egg production hugely, and its fibre was woven into huckabuck, which was stronger, warmer and whiter than Irish linen and preferred by cottagers, especially for towels and tablecloths.

Another multi-purpose cottage plant was the elder: it could be set for a very quick-growing hedge if you wanted to claim a patch of land as a squatter, for example, as cuttings struck root in no time at all and it soon produced strong shoots. The berries were the basis of many a country wine

that some said was as good as any made from grapes; the flowers could be distilled for gently scented toilet water, or made into wines and lemonades, or fried as fritters, or used with the leaves as the essential ingredient of many herbal ointments. Elder wood was ideal for shoemaker's pegs, butcher's skewers, angling rods and mathematical instruments; it was used a lot by turners and toymakers, and the young stems were beloved by schoolchildren who removed the central pith to make pea-shooters and whistles.

Hawthorn was another well loved tree or bush: quite apart from being the universal thorny hedge plant, you could make may-blossom wine or eat young hawthorn leaves, or make tea from them by rinsing fresh leaves in cold water, steaming them until they turned an olive-green and then drying them on the hot-plate. The native crab apple was another favourite, not only for jellies but also for the fruit's verjuice, or varges, which was used on sprains.

Mr and Mrs Clark sawing firewood in Sussex, early 20th century.

So many plants, in the garden or in the wild, served so many purposes. Teasels, which grow at their own whim all over my own cottage garden, were originally a carefully grown crop, harvested for those thistle-like heads which were used for raising the nap on woollen cloth. Furze, or gorse, offered a lot more than the rich scent and colour of its golden flowers: it was used by dyers, it was grown as an impenetrable short-term hedge, it was cut for fuel (gorse ash makes a good alkaline fertilizer) and also cut and bruised to be fed to livestock – the 'salt' in the plant was said to give animals a clear skin.

The lucky few had enough ground for an orchard but most cottagers planted fruit trees if they had any space at all – often one of everything for variety. There were apples of every kind, of course (and here again the huge list of old names is pure poetry); some even used apples for apple bread – one third boiled apple pulp baked with two thirds flour (the dough fermented with yeast for twelve hours before entering the oven). There were pear trees, cherry trees, damsons, greengages (first introduced in the 1720s) and the ubiquitous Victoria plum. Older gardens might have the proper quince with its lingering aroma, and medlars (eaten only when rotting) and mulberry bushes. There were always blackcurrant bushes – so easy to grow – and probably red and white currants too, and there were always gooseberries, grown for local competitions as much as for home consumption – Baxter mentions between 700 and 800 varieties of gooseberry. And raspberries and, for those who could take the care, strawberries, though many simply harvested wild ones.

For much of the 19th century, wild harvesting was still a way of life – mushrooms, blackberries, sloes, rowan berries, hazel nuts (though you could grow cultivated varieties like Bond nut, cob nut, Cosford nut, Lambert's nut, Pearson's Prolific or Barcelona nut) and walnuts, which you gathered ripe from a forgotten garden and let ferment in a heap for a few days to separate the green case from the nut, staining your fingers black.

The wild plants were the cottager's herb garden. Precious garden space might be given to sweet culinary herbs like knotted marjoram, parsley, sage, summer savory, tarragon, basil, fennel, blue hyssop, balm, bergamot, lavender, rosemary, mint and thyme, but those for medicinal and other purposes were mainly gathered from the hedgerows and meadows. There were endless sources of dye colours, for example, and there were aptly named plants like soapwort and butcher's broom.

However, Richard Jefferies, writing in the 1870s, noticed that the old country knowledge of herbalism had already been lost in most villages. Elderflower ointment persisted, and was sold in town shops – but without its magic ingredient of a little piece of adder's-tongue fern, which made all the difference between the apothecary's recipe and the wise woman's. Some cottagers were still using silgreen, or sengreen, the common houseleek

(*Sempervivum tectorum*) that grew on the cottage itself, as a cure for wounds, burns and stings: they bruised the plant's leaves and mixed the resulting pulp and juice with cream. Others used tobacco juice on cuts and had forgotten older remedies like knotted figwort. And though the shops did a roaring trade in iron tonics, some country people still relied on the old custom of dropping an iron nail into wine, sherry or cider as a restorative but had probably forgotten the value of willow bark as a tonic for debility and a cure for pain (it is the basis of aspirin). Could any of them remember the virtues of weeds like loving-andrews (the blue meadow geranium), loggerums (knapweed and scabious), Saturday night's pepper (spurge) or gran'fer goslings (spotted-leaf orchis)? What about using bluebell juice for starch? Did they make their cheeks rosier by rubbing them with primrose leaves? What about cleaning teeth with sage leaves or a cut strawberry (which would also whiten the skin), or relieving itches with pansy leaves, using lily-root ointments for boils or rubbing onions on chilblains (with salt) or on a bald head (with honey)? Or trapping birds with bird-lime from the juice of a holly tree?

There were so many remedies, many based perhaps more on faith and superstition than on the real healing powers of herbs, though these can often be proven even to the satisfaction of modern scientists. Most seemed to be for the treatment of coughs and colds, rheumatism, bladder and bowel problems, indigestion and warts – everyday problems of that kind. Honey was used for coughs, colds and sore throats but it was only one of countless aids – many added horehound as an expectorant and tonic; used a tisane of marjoram to fight a cold; blackcurrant jelly for the throat; liquorice as a demulcent for catarrh; linseed tea for chest diseases; a gargle of sage and vinegar with honey; hollyhocks for lung problems, coltsfoot for a chesty cough (and also as substitute tobacco) and mullein for various respiratory ailments.

Radishes helped with bladder problems (and were a magical cure for warts and corns); juniper berries and dandelions were good diuretics, and so were hops – the all-purpose plant was used not only in brewing (before its introduction from Flanders, the English had used ground ivy or germander to preserve beer) but also as a recognized narcotic: the scent of hop flowers is soporific and even George III used a hop-filled pillow to ease pain and get a good night's sleep. Lettuce juice was dried and used as a mild opiate, and violets were also sleep aids – but you had to be wary of bringing them into the house as decorative flowers, because it was said that they carried fleas on their stems! However, you could then burn some fleabane to get rid of the pests (or use the plant before you burned it to scour wooden tables and floors). Dried tansy flowers or hanging bunches of southernwood were used as general domestic insect repellents, while the mullein's powdery leaf-down was death to cockroaches; hollyhock flowers guarded the cottage against invasion by fleas and lice, dried lavender deterred moths and a tincture made from delphinium seeds dealt with head nits. In the garden, tobacco killed off aphids if soap suds were too precious for the job.

Spiders, however, were useful. A child with whooping-cough would have a bag of live spiders tied round its neck, poor little thing, and pills made of spider's web were used as tranquillizers. More important (and valid) was the use of web to staunch wounds – that really works. Other wound dressings included yarrow as a blood-clotting agent (it was also said that yarrow flowers and leaves could cure baldness), witch hazel as a styptic, and lily root or primrose leaves for burns, boils and ulcers. Comfrey was an acknowledged knitter of broken bones, and the pretty little eyebright was so named for its juice's powers to soothe sore eyes.

Sore tums were treated with peppermint oil or rosemary (whose leaves were also useful as a brunette's hair rinse). Mulberry syrup or medlars were good laxatives, a teaspoonful of mustard seeds did wonders for dyspepsia, and blackberries reduced diarrhoea. Chamomile was an all-purpose herb for poorly stomachs, indigestion, flatulence, loss of appetite, constipation and a general tonic and sedative.

Many country people seemed to suffer from rheumatism, gout and arthritis, and they set about treating themselves with ground elder, raspberries, primroses or the juice of daisy leaves. The latter was also sniffed by migraine sufferers, though others might try auricula for headaches. Every cottage had its own cures for the ills of its inhabitants, and most of the ingredients were to be found for free in the countryside or were deliberately grown in the practical garden.

There were flowers, too, of course, grown initially for the same reasons as herbs but increasingly for pure pleasure, too, especially during the Victorian age, though often confined to dead-straight beds on either side of the path that ran from the lane to the cottage door. Many became specialists in certain species or varieties, and it is said that gardeners today owe a great deal to the cottagers and artisans who took such a pride in growing and breeding all manner of flowering plants. Dahlias, first introduced from Mexico in 1789 and introduced again in 1804, were fast growing in popularity during the 1830s. The most widely grown cottage flower during the late 18th century was probably the polyanthus and it was soon joined by auricula, ranunculus, aubrieta, solomon's seal, gladiolus, geranium, anemone, carnation, pansy, stocks of every kind, bright cornflowers, a rainbow of tulips and a brilliant sunset of nasturtiums. (Did you know, incidentally, that nasturtium flowers spontaneously emit visible sparks at intervals in the evening? Neither did I, but Baxter claims so.) But in fact, as with herbs, country cottagers had such a plethora of wildflowers in the meadows, woods and hedgerows that they scarcely needed to bother with garden flowers except for those who could not resist the increasing fascination with breeding new varieties, a craze which swept through every level of society.

The really passionate crammed flowers in everywhere, mingling them with the vegetables. Gertrude Jekyll, a landscape gardener by profession, describes with delight a tiny front garden in which the cottager had built rough wooden staging which was completely smothered with flowering pot plants, kept in a miniscule homemade greenhouse during severe weather – though goodness knows where he kept the continual supply of new plants that regularly took their place on the staging at their peak flowering season so that the whole area was constantly in bloom. They included fuchsias, geraniums, begonias, lilies, hydrangeas, francoa and countless half-hardy annuals, and a clematic scrambling exuberantly over the little porch.

Some plants were essentially cottage garden ones – the annual fiery display of vivid nasturtiums, scented biennials like sweet william and wallflower, carefully bred varieties of auricula, canterbury bells and delphiniums, tender favourites like dahlias and china asters (or 'chaney oysters') grown for the village show, and, of course, the reliable rose-pink flowers of the everlasting pea or winter bean. Honeysuckle and 'jessamy' (jasmine) sprawled where they would, mingling with the roses – old types of double white, or pink Maiden's Blush, floriferous cluster roses and great swathes of banksia on the walls.

And on the windowsills, almost hidden by the roses that rambled and clambered over the cottage, would be proudly displayed pot plants including cactus, lily and vermilion pelargoniums (or, as the poet Louis Macneice put it, 'the country cot with a pot of pink geraniums') beside jars brimming with picked wildflowers – bluebells, meadow orchids, cowslips and ox eye daisies. The garden and the countryside were welcomed right into the cottage itself.

J. Mantell, FLS, wrote during the 1830s: 'For who can pass even the poor man's cot, where the hand of industry has tastefully entwined the rose, the honeysuckle, and the briar around the very threshold of his home, without associating in his mind the idea of comfort, of happiness within; but if the weeds of indolence are seen towering in luxuriant growth over the loveliest gems of Flora's Temple, choking up, as it were, the very approaches of the habitation, who will not, with emotions of regret, conclude that waste and prodigality are the inmates there. How important is it then to induce a taste for the cultivation of flowers!'

Mary Russell Mitford, born in 1787, was much less floribund but wrote lyrically of country gardens and I cannot resist quoting from her descriptions of a Berkshire village in the 1820s. First, she describes her own family's little home, saying that 'the pride of my heart and the delight of my eyes is my garden,' though the house itself was 'in dimensions very much like a bird-cage, and might, with almost equal convenience, be laid on a shelf, or hung up in a tree.' Without the garden, the house was unbearably small in warm weather, but outside there were vines, cherry-trees full of birds' nests, China roses covering the walls, honeysuckles and jasmine, big clusters of tall hollyhocks, a magnificent bay tree and a huge old elder tree, butterflies dancing attendance on the dahlias and bee-hawkmoths hovering over the rich geraniums, a tangle of convolvulus, lilies, heart's-ease and mignonette smothering the tiny gravel paths.

'A cottage – no – a miniature house, with many additions, little odds and ends of places, pantries, and what not; all angles, and of a charming in-and-outness; a little bricked court before one half, and a little flower-yard before the other; the walls, old and weather-stained, covered with hollyhocks, roses, honey-suckles, and a great apricot-tree; the casements full of geraniums; (ah, there is our superb white cat peeping out from amongst them); the closets (our landlord has the assurance to call them rooms) full of contrivances and corner-cupboards; and the little garden behind full of common flowers, tulips, pinks, larkspurs, peonies, stocks, and carnations, with an arbour of privet, not unlike a sentry-box, where one lives in a delicious green light, and looks out on the gayest of all gay flower-beds.'

— 4 —

COLOURING THE OUTLINE

An elderly gentleman (and I use the word carefully) living in an elegant early 18th century house asked for my help in delving into the history of his fine home, especially the personalities of its past occupants. We tapped many sources; we waded through deeds and mortgage documents, local history papers, court rolls, census returns, old trade directories and suchlike, and from these we could learn many basic facts. But we wanted to bring the characters to life and to *feel* them living in the house. We had one particularly lucky break in that the original owner in the early 18th century had been a man of position in the service of a bishop, and some of the letters he had written concerning his daily affairs were still held at the county record office. We asked a graphologist to analyse the man's handwriting and an intriguing picture began to emerge – his character, his physique and even his state of health at different times. We managed to track down a portrait of his brother, who had been Lord Mayor of London, and found that the latter's hefty weight and facial features seemed to tally admirably with the graphologist's word portrait of our hero: there was a decided family likeness.

Cottage dwellers rarely leave much documentary evidence of their lives, though you might be lucky enough to hear the memories of old folk recalling tales of their neighbours told by their own grandparents and begin to build up your picture thus. You might come across a little cache of objects here and there in the cottage and garden – money, of course, and old newspapers or perhaps items deliberately built into the walls or chimney as charms to protect the cottage and its inhabitants. Typical among such objects are shoes, sacrificed chickens and anti-witch devices like pins and knives.

But there is another area of clues you can trace, one which we also used in that 18th-century house. We looked at the paintwork. We took a small piece of wood panelling from behind a window seat and very carefully rubbed it down to reveal successive layers of paint. Then, working on the principle that people tend to redecorate when they first move in or when there is a marriage, and referring also to period fashions, we began to work out which inhabitant had chosen which colour and how that might have reflected their personalities.

Cottagers, of course, did not necessarily have access to such a wide choice of paint colours – they were unlikely, perhaps, to use some of the very subtle shades we found in that house – but you can still enjoy literally peeling back the painted layers of time to get an idea of what the cottage was like at different stages by working on the woodwork and also, less easily, the wall distemper. There are pitfalls: undercoats can be confused with top coats, and anyway some colours fade or even change completely with age. But you might well be in for a vivid surprise. For a start, think of the difference when an old oil painting is professionally cleaned: what had been dark and dingy springs brightly to life and colour. Old stone walls, when first built, might have been as bright as the newly scrubbed Houses of Parliament are today; and the woodwork of a cottage was very likely as fresh and clean as a newly hewn log until later fashions covered it with paints and stains.

For a decade I lived in a small, tile-hung brick cottage, some two centuries old, with exposed beams in the livingroom and a good inglenook. When I first moved in, most of the woodwork was black (deep skirting-boards, beams, floorboards and staircase) while the window frames and internal doors were a sickly cream. Sanding down the skirting-boards and stairs, I discovered that at one stage they had all been a harsh, primary green, and beneath that a dreary chocolate brown and, to my surprise, before that an equally primary red. The hair-and-plaster walls, under later emulsions, had been whitewashed and at one stage colour-washed an amazing hot pink, quickly veiled with dark cream. The kitchen walls had once been contrasting – two in bright blue and two in bright yellow.

Cottagers could be quite imaginative with their decorations. Red ochre bands decorated some 19th-century Ulster cottages, for example; in northern English counties there was a cottage fashion for a deep blue limewash, while others preferred yellow ochre and in Derbyshire it seems they liked a light green based on copperas.

Limewashes were the traditional finish on external earth or wattle-and-daub walls – think of the reds, pinks and ochres of certain regions. In the West Country, for example, cob was given a colourwash to protect its mud, with a band of pitch at ground level. The finish is basically quicklime slaked with water; you can add a binding agent like animal tallow or raw linseed oil to give better weather protection (the old way was to put waste animal fat and lime into a tub and then pour on boiling water to melt the fat and slake the lime) or add milk or curds for their casein, which can be smelly but the casein forms a reasonably insoluble compound with the lime and helps to prevent the rain washing off the lime dust.

Indoors it was cheaper and easier to use whitewash made from crushed chalk powder mixed with water, adding size (often starch) as a binding agent – and that, broadly, is distemper. It was far from weatherproof and tended to become a dust which brushed off easily so that it had to be constantly reapplied. But new whitewash made the place look so fresh, and limewash had the added advantage of being a good disinfectant.

Various pigments could be added to the basic white. Pink limewashes, for example, were made by mixing the quicklime with a brick-red mineral oxide. Potash with sulphur made a greenish grey, and some local clays could give yellows and browns. Sulphate of copper with milk of lime produced lime-blue; verdigris (cupric acetate or carbonate) a greenish-blue. Red and yellow earth ochres were common and were also used to make patterns, as was lampblack. Oil paints, based on linseed oil with various turpentines, were less easy to use and, for a cottager, much less affordable, though many used stains including a reddish one said to have been based on bull's blood and red ochre. Distempered cottage walls were sometimes decorated with stencilled work, especially in the pre-Victorian decades. You could well find that your cottage's interior was far more colourful than you might expect.

Wallpaper was a luxury because of a tax on paper up to the mid 19th century, after which it gradually became cheaper than stencilling. But cottagers might cover their walls with wood panelling – not in an attempt to mimic gentry fashions but, like the gentry, as a practical means of hiding all that pervasive rising damp and to provide a little insulation against its accompanying cold dankness. Cottagers could not afford durable woods like oak and their softwood panels did not last very long.

They also covered their walls with pictures, especially cheap prints (Dick Turpin, biblical scenes and lurid battle scenes seemed to be favourites), samplers (worked on perforated cardboard if they could not afford the proper canvas), appliqué pictures, and calendar pictures depicting royalty or the works of Constable and Turner in particular. Jefferies tells of a tiny cottage, its one room beautifully maintained by its very poor inhabitants who had completely covered the walls with etchings carefully cut from the pages of the *Illustrated London News*.

Photography was invented early in the Victorian period but it was of course a long while before cottagers could afford to decorate their homes with family snapshots. But they could – and did – fill their mantelshelves with bits and bobs galore.

A farmhouse kitchen in
Radnorshire.

FURNITURE AND THINGS

Wood was the traditional material for so many household items while there
were still craftsmen living in the village and in the woodlands who worked
in that medium, turning bowls and spoons or coopering iron-banded
washtubs and storage vessels using the same techniques as for making barrels
and casks. Every fieldworker had a small, personal cask for ale or cider in
the field. Wooden trenchers were common as dinner plates; cups, spoons,
boxes and combs were fashioned from the horns of cattle and sheep – a
material which was as malleable as any modern plastic if you knew how to

handle it. Wooden utensils were easy enough to mend if they cracked with age: you simply soaked them to swell the wood and close the gap, securing the join with a bit of metal, or you tapped in some strategic wooden wedges. If you wanted a wooden vessel to be waterproof you could wax or grease it – yet another use for animal fat (think of candles, soap, limewash and other household applications, quite apart from cooking, and you can understand why livestock breeders of the 18th and 19th centuries concentrated on breeding grossly fat animals).

Then, before cottage vessels nearly all became enamelled metal, the most common material was probably redware (glazed red earthenware) used for making large containers or 'redpans', often with big wooden lids with a handle on top. They were used mainly for storing bread and also as washing bowls for dishes and laundry. A big redpan might be placed in the built-in wooden scullery sink, or stood on four thick, square-cut logs so that you did not have to bend down too far as you washed. During the rest of the week the same redpan might be used for other tasks such as winemaking.

Redware was also popular for the large pitchers in which well water was fetched, and for lard-pots and the round, lipped pipkins used in cooking, each with a straight handle projecting at a slight angle on one side. A paler Dorset clay was used here and there for fat, round harvest-bottles, their yellow-glazed necks and shoulders bearing two little ears to take a carrying cord or thong.

Stoneware was popular, too: it was a good, hard material for bottles, jugs, tobacco jars, flagons, food storage, slow-cook pipkins, and mugs – including dog-handled tavern mugs with three handles so that a single precious mug could be passed round and there would be three different places for people's lips. Some of the best stoneware was made in the North and the Midlands and found its way all over the country, transported by canal in the early 19th century. Some preferred Bristolware, which was part buff and part yellowish brown and remained very popular until about the 1860s or 1870s. Others liked dipped ware – mugs, jugs and basins which might have a yellow-buff ground with bands of white decorated with blue, brown and green, or white striped with brown, black and blue or more subtle colours, and there were often trees in the design. Then there was painted ware and of course there was also the cottage favourite: willow-pattern plates in blue and white which were often proudly displayed on the dresser, or the same colours for English country landscapes, which frequently featured cows. Lustre ware was commonly bought or won at fairgrounds, its copper lustre perhaps combined with coloured decorations, or in contrast the absolutely plain colour of Wedgwood blackware. White Staffordshireware, decorated with farm implements and mottos, was a farmhouse favourite.

And every cottage dresser and mantelpiece had its china ornaments, often bought at the fair. There were toby-jugs, cow-and-milkmaid jugs, assorted figurines, spotted dogs and cats, little houses and flower-holders; scattered among them would be brass pepper-pots, pewter salt-cellars, brass or carved wooden spoons, children's fairground moneyboxes in china or earthenware or wood, and perhaps a few natural knick-knacks like a roe buck's antler found in the woods, a jay's tiny blue striped feather, an unusual pebble or shell, a sea-urchin fossil or a knapped flint. And there might be a lacquered papier-mâché tray with flowers painted against a black background and decorated with little pieces of mother-of-pearl, or some precious objects passed to the cottagers from 'better' houses like the vicarage or even the manor house – the remnants of a divided set, or items which were cracked or chipped such as porcelain, engraved glass, pewter, a plated candlestick, an old hourglass, all sorts of little boxes and maybe even a mirror over the chimneypiece.

The hourglass gave way to clocks, especially once the railway network had become well established after the middle of the 19th century. Before, people kept local time and relied on the church clock or the sun or their bellies; but when railway timetables were introduced it was suddenly necessary for everybody to keep the same time, rather than it being six o'clock in a part of Bedfordshire when it was sevenish in Leicester.

Lakeland kitchen in Keswick with a fine old dresser and homemade stool.

The cheapest cottage timepieces were the very pretty 'Dutch' clocks, each with a white dial painted with bunches of flowers, the weights dangling below on dainty chains and fully revealed as there was no case to hide them. Grandfather clocks were found in farmhouses during the 18th century and even in a few cottages by the early 19th – clocks that only needed winding every eight days. More affordable were cottage 24-hour clocks in their plainer oak long-cases. Jefferies said that there were 'eight-day clocks standing in tall, square oaken cases by the staircase in the cottage' and that these were generally picked up as bargains at farmhouse sales when farm tenancies came to an end, especially during the 19th-century leave-the-land trend when many farming families saw their sons opting to go into trade instead.

For a cottage, declared Jefferies, 'the furniture required is not much, but there must be some.' The farmhouse sales were the source for numerous formal sideboards, old chairs, large oak or maple bedsteads with good feather beds and blankets – furniture far more substantial than you might expect in a cottage and items which had probably been in the farmhouse for several generations before filtering down to the cottagers, who would carefully hand selected pieces over to their children when a young couple first married and set up their own home.

The early cottagers had three main problems in furnishing their homes: lack of space, lack of means and, finally, uneven floors. They solved the latter problem quite simply by using three-legged stools, chairs and tables. As every barnyard milker knows, three legs stand true where four legs are irritatingly tipsy. Try it for yourself, in the garden perhaps. A three-legged stool or table will stand firm without needing any balancing chocks.

Stools preceded chairs. Bear in mind, of course, that cottagers did not sit around very often; by day they were usually out of the home, working in the fields or wherever, and at the end of all that they were often tired enough to go straight to bed after a meal, especially when the evenings were darkly long. So they perched on stools or on rough benches rather than lounging against chair-backs.

The simplest bench was merely a plank or slab of wood with short, rough legs knocked into gouged-out holes. The most sought-after bench was right inside the inglenook and here the ends of a thick plank were simply bedded into the wall, with no need for supporting legs. Before the 19th century, the typical one-room country cottage usually had just a few benches, around the hearth and against the walls, which were used for sleeping as well as sitting, and but one table – and that was it. Even in grander places, they would remove the boards from the trestle tables after eating and put them on the floor for sleepers.

During the 19th century, what had previously been good yeoman farmhouses descended the social scale and were described as cottages, as they are today. They had at least two downstairs rooms and there was more room for furniture, though it often remained sparse and functional until ideas began to filter down from better houses – and not just ideas. Some employers and squires would pass on secondhand furniture in recognition of good service, perhaps, and apart from Jefferies's farmhouse sales there were also some bargains to be had in village stores which stocked 'antique' furniture, or at the fairs and markets, where a cottager might find something which was relatively cheap because it was 'old-fashioned'. By then, of course, chairs had long become cottage essentials and had initially followed the principles of stool-making: the backs were of round sticks driven into slab-wood seats. The ubiquitous Windsor chair was more refined: its sticks were produced by turners and its seat was sculpted to a comfortable shape for buttocks by craftsmen wielding adzes. Bentwood chairs were simpler and cheaper to make, as long as craftsmen retained the art of steaming wood to curve it into chair-backs and seat frames, but Windsors were favourites.

Rush, straw and cane were typical materials for cottage furniture, too, and offered craft opportunities for those who had the skills to make and mend in them. Wickerwork principles applied equally to baskets and to furniture, and the raw material might be at its crudest hazel rods or osiers, or later round and split cane. By the last quarter of the 19th century, wicker armchairs by the fire represented the height of cottage sophistication.

Rushwork was much more comfortable to sit on than plain wood for the millions who could not afford upholstery, and it was cheap enough where locally available for rush-bottomed stools, hassocks and ladder-back chairs. Straw, the basis of the major cottage industry of straw-plaiting for bonnet makers in the early 19th century, was also twisted into ropes which could then be fashioned into truckle beds, cradles and cosy, draughtproof 'beehive' chairs as well as genuine beehives. The method, known as lipwork, involved coiling the ropes into the required form and binding them in place. The truckle bed was a simple enough piece to make – usually for a shepherd or as a quick extra bed at an inn: you formed the rope into a flat mat big enough to fit your body and then continued it vertically for a couple of rounds to make a draught-excluding lip that also retained your bedclothes. The coils were usually held together with light, pointed little sticks. Beehive chairs were more elaborate: you began by making a drum shape, much like a rush hassock, and then continued up the sides and back above the seat, arching over the sitter's head in a warm, protective half-cocoon. Some people devised similar shapes based less comfortably on recycled barrels.

Draughtproofing was essential; every cottage was alive with draughts, and anyway often needed draughts and openings to get rid of the fire smoke. So you took care to sit protected from the draughts if you could. Apart from hooded beehive chairs, there were solidly high-backed settles (some of them converting into beds or chests) and there were screens and partitions in case the strips of dad's old trousers nailed to the doorframe failed to plug the gaps. Jefferies noted that many late 19th century cottages were fitted with wooden screens, dividing already small rooms into two, 'the outer of which, towards the door, is a howling wilderness of draught and wet from under the door; and the inner part close, stuffy, and dim with smoke driven down the chimney by the shifting wind. Here the family are all huddled up together close over the embers. Here they sit in the dark, or in such light as is supplied by the carefully hoarded stock of fuel, till it is time to go to bed.'

If you sat, protected from draughts, in your inglenook, you could easily reach little niches in the wall for your clay pipe. This cheap luxury was very beautiful in its delicate simplicity and many cottage gardens still yield tantalizing pieces of white clay pipes – usually broken stems – when the vegetable patch is dug over; somehow they seem to come to the surface almost of their own accord. They were made almost as soon as tobacco was first landed in England in the late 1550s and were used by women and children as well as men. The earliest were probably based on designs similar to the pipes smoked for medicinal and cultural reasons by the American Indians and were even tinier than the slender little ones you are most likely to find. In Victorian times, clay pipes were produced so cheaply and on such a large scale that they were often given away by the village pub, or you could buy them by the gross.

Most of the pipe-clay came from the south-western counties, though occasionally small deposits could be found locally. The same white clay was used for making cleaning materials such as hearth-stone. The pipes were made by hand-rolling clay balls into an approximate pipe shape (bowl and stem all in one), then inserting a brass or steel piercing rod with a diameter of an eighth of an inch or less down the stem before putting the whole into a mould and using a press to create the bowl hollow. There were many fashions for decorating bowls, but most cottagers were content with the plain type. The finished mouldings were stacked and fired in a kiln; after cooling, the mouthpieces would be polished or protected with soap, gum, sealing wax or (later) lacquer so that they did not stick to the lips. If a cottager found the stem too long for comfort, he simply snapped it off where convenient and dipped the new end in tea or beer to make up for the loss of the protective finish on the mouthpiece.

Such a pipe could last a long time if you cleaned it by putting it into the fire's hot embers, and dedicated smokers kept iron pipe-racks for that purpose. Most of the pipes you will find today were made before the Great War, though they were still being made for connoisseurs of the cool, slow smoke right up until 1989 or later.

William Cobbett, the labourers' champion, frequently addressed cottage life and sought to improve what he often found appalling. He noted, for example, the Leicestershire village of Knighton with its hovels made of mud and straw, 'bits of glass or of old cast-off windows, without frames or hinges frequently, but merely stuck in the mud walls.' These hovels were furnished with 'bits of chairs and stools, a few wretched boards tacked together to form a table, a miserable make-shift for a bed.' In typically emphatic language, he wrote in his *Cottage Economy* tracts: 'In *household goods*, the *warm*, the *strong*, the *durable*, ought always to be kept in view. Oak tables, bedsteads and stocks, chairs of oak or of yew-tree, and never a bit of miserable deal board. Things of this sort ought to last several lifetimes. A labourer ought to inherit from his great grandfather something besides his toil . . . In short, when a house is once furnished with sufficient goods, there ought to be no renewal of hardly any part of them wanted for half an age, except in case of destruction by fire.'

English cottagers had traditionally used oak furniture (or perhaps ash, elm or fruit-tree wood, depending on what was locally available); in Scotland, in contrast, pine and fir were the main furniture timbers. But during the 19th century huge quantities of the 'miserable deal board' so abhorred by Cobbett were pouring into England from Scandinavia and being turned into cheap, mass-produced furniture. Gertrude Jekyll agreed with Cobbett and noted with regret how rare the solid old country furniture had become by the end of the 19th century, even in farmhouses. She laid the blame on 'straining after a kind of display unsuited to station' and also the bad influence of 'the quantity of cheap rubbish, the outcome of trade competition, offered in shops; stuff that has no use or beauty, but that is got up for rapid sale with a showy exterior in imitation of a class of appointment used in houses of an entirely different class.' Yet here and there she came across farmers and cottagers who had resisted such 'pretentious frivolity' and retained the benched tables of thick oak (perfect boards for wooden trenchers and horn mugs), flapped parlour tables, three-legged tables, table-topped elm stools, oaken cottage dressers, and oak linen hutches and clothes hutches which also acted as seats. During the earlier years of the 20th century, many cottages and farmhouses in more remote areas became goldmines for antique dealers.

The fact remained that cottages were essentially small and did not have much space for furniture, though some positively stuffed their rooms with it if they could. Storage, of course, was at a premium. The hutches or chests for storing linen and clothes sometimes had a loose tray under the lid, but chests of drawers were rare in cottages until well into the 19th century. And then there were cupboards – little cupboards built into convenient nooks and crannies, set into solid walls, tucked in beside the chimney to keep precious commodities like salt and spices dry. There were ventilated cupboards for storing foods, perhaps with wickerwork panels or wooden slats and rods to admit air while excluding rodents. Clothes remained in hutches, however, rather than in wardrobes.

Cupboards were for hiding things; dressers, on the other hand, boldly displayed as well as stored the best crockery and usually also acted as sideboards. Dressers were in virtually every cottage in the 19th century. They might be simply a set of shelves set between a pair of vertical planks, with nothing but the bare house wall or room partition at the back; they might be proper pieces of free-standing furniture with a sideboard base (fitted with cupboards or drawers) and a set of shelves above against a back board. Whichever, they generally had pride of place in the main living-room/kitchen, and sometimes formed a screen to make a sleeping area as well. While farmhouse dressers might be of good hardwoods like oak, cottage ones were usually of softwoods – the ubiquitous 19th century deal.

There is one thing about English cottages that immediately strikes many Europeans – the lack of colourful decoration on the furniture. Although the old cottagers might paint their Windsor chairs in one colour, such as primary blue or green, there was none of that lovely floral decoration you can still find in countries like Poland, for example. I know of Poles who came to England during the war and were immediately struck by the lack of lively colour and pattern in English homes – no elaborately painted wood-burning stoves or tiles or cupboards or chests of drawers, nor had there been since the end of the 17th century. But cottagers had touches of bright colour and pattern in the ribbons some used to tie back window curtains, or perhaps a bright and flowery American tablecloth, or patchwork quilts on the beds or shielding the front door.

BEDS AND BEDROOMS

In the old one-room cottage, the bed was usually as close to the fire as possible and was either curtained off or boxed off in an alcove, not so much for privacy as for warmth. Typical was the bed closet – literally a bed in a cupboard with wooden doors (with or without ventilation) so that you could shut yourself in and build up a really good fug in your box, as snug as a ferret in its nest. Such bed cupboards, often free-standing, were still being made after Victoria came to the throne. Sometimes a bed closet was built as an outshut under its own little lean-to roof and this might be the only section of roof that was lined – to prevent bits of thatch and thatchlife from dropping down on the sleepers. There might be just some sacking pinned in place, or whitewashed newspaper, or carefully woven mats made from straw or grass or rushes.

One-room home with smokehood, and a bed alcove with a lined roof above it.

The theme persisted when beds moved up under the main roof – when a sleeping platform was created at eaves level across one end of the main room by laying a few gappy planks over crossbeams resting on the tops of the walls, perhaps. You clambered bedwards up a near-vertical ladder to reach this loft, like making for the top bunk in a night-train or a ship's cabin.

And you had plenty of company in bed. A woman recalling her teenage years in the early 19th century, in the model Dorset village of Milton Abbas, said that the family lived in two downstairs rooms (there was another family in the cottage's upstairs rooms) and shared two beds – mother and father in one, two girls and a boy (all teenagers) in the other. In another one-up, one-down cottage nearby, a family of eleven all slept in the same upstairs room – three girls, six boys and the parents. They were in some ways lucky; many of the village's families lived wholly in one room, with but a curtain between the beds for a vestige of privacy.

Beds were shared partly to economize on beds and space, and partly for warmth. I remember spending the coldest night of my life in an ordinary English cottage – the winter weather was not that bad but the bedroom and bed were as cold as the grave, a penetrating cold that had me literally shivering and sleepless all night long. Perhaps what I had needed was a nice copper warming-pan, lined inside with iron to take charcoal or hot wood embers, or – in the luxury of large farm beds – a 'bed waggon', which consisted of a sheet of iron supporting a trivet into which a pan of hot embers was placed. Another sheet of iron was above the trivet and the whole thing was caged in rails and oval hoops of oak to lift the bedclothes clear of the source of heat while the bed was being warmed. Naturally the smouldering contraption was removed before the bed was occupied.

'Bed waggon' to warm a large bed with hot embers.

No wonder cottagers used to encourage their daughters in the traditional pastime of 'bundling' – a young couple would go to bed together, keeping warm and getting to know each other to a certain extent, but with the practical precaution that the girl's mother would have bound her legs together or literally stitched her into an all-embracing skirt like a sack, or would have placed a bolster between the pair as a far from certain method of birth control!

For a long time mattresses were no more than straw or dried bracken or even dry autumn leaves, at first loose and then covered with coarse linen cloth and finally bagged in some way. The stuff had the advantage of being warm and was easily replaced when it became sordid (women usually gave birth on straw mattresses for that reason) but it also harboured all sorts of dust and creepy-crawlies, and offered a nesting haven for mice. Sometimes the mattress was simply placed on the floor; sometimes it was supported on a cradle of straw ropes suspended from a frame, or on wooden slats. Babies might be lucky enough to sleep on the softer filling of fresh chaff, hoarded by a farmworker after threshing and winnowing, within its own plain wooden cradle. Flock (waste wool – very lumpy) was another mattress filling, and so was horsehair, tightly twisted into cords and then boiled, dried and chopped up so that it formed curls. Feather beds, however, became more common, often laid on a thick straw mattress for added insulation. It was said that sailors had been sleeping on feather beds even in medieval times because they doubled up as life rafts: the feathers were encased in waxen linen and were virtually unsinkable should the ship capsize – the sleeping sailor simply drifted out to sea . . .

Those who had plenty of poultry made their own feather pillows, carefully drying the feathers in a very slow oven overnight but making sure they did not include a bird's flight feathers. These were said to make the sleeper restless as they were 'flighty' – and anyway their sharp ends poked through the pillowcase.

Bed linen was originally just that – coarse linen cloths laid over the straw (which remained scratchy) and over your body. Sheets came into cottages during the second half of the 19th century, and they were precious indeed: many people remember (and still practise) the economy of turning worn sheets sides-to-middle to give them new life. Mavis Budd remembers, in the 1920s, the special and intense joy of sleeping in new blankets, fingering them, stroking them, smelling them and 'trying to reconcile myself to the fact that they actually belonged to us, to my sisters and me, and they were not second-hand, or borrowed, or in any way a gift of compassion.' She remembers, too, her grandparents' bedroom, reached by a dark, narrow, winding stairway with creaking triangular treads. The rooms were always cold, each smelling distinctively of its inhabitants; there were mountainous feather mattresses on the beds, with soft, fringed white covers down to the lino-covered oak floorboards (hiding the chamberpot under the bed), lots of over-bright flowery mats and rag rugs, and bamboo bedside tables stained with cough mixture and candle grease. Her grandparents' bedroom, its window never opened, reeked mustily of camphor, lavender and mothballs.

Most late Victorian and early 20th-century women liked to have pretty things in their cottage bedrooms, especially flowered china bits and pieces like trinket trays, washing bowls and ewers or rose-and-poppy chamberpots, even if they had to sleep on an iron bedstead rather than a fine brass one or a wooden four-poster. Being poorer than average did not stop them from expressing their creativity and taste.

CLOTHES

Spoilt for choice, cottagers were not. Clothes were largely homemade, knitted or hand-stitched if they could afford to buy new material, which many could not; or they were second-hand bargains, or cast-off gifts from the manor and the parson. Clothes were kept going to their last shred and were worn until there was no more material to hold the darns and patches together. Women's hands were never still; they would be pulling worn-out woollies to pieces and knitting them into stockings, or darning socks and longjohns seats and jumpers and sheets, or turning worn sheets sides-to-middle and eventually cutting up the sides to make pillowcases, using the worst of the latter as dish cloths. Exhausted flannel petticoats became floor cloths, needed in endless supplies as the cottage floors and wooden tables were scrubbed and rubbed from end to end every Friday. Nobody actually bought cloths, though gypsies sold tea cloths as well as towels, aprons, rolls of material, wooden clothes pegs and countless skeins of darning wool (tuppence a skein in the 1920s).

Materials for clothes were from animal and plant sources: sheep's wool which, long ago, had been spun at home; linen from flax, spun and often woven at home into the 19th century; and cotton, imported from the East in the 18th century, the ready-spun threads of which formed the basis of a cottage weaving industry until large factory looms began to put cottage handlooms out of business during the 19th century. Cotton was also imported already woven as calico, which could be worn in its plain state, bleached or not, or printed.

Several major cottage industries had been concerned with the production of clothing materials, directly or indirectly, and some lasted through most of the 19th century – especially glove-making, in which cottagers in due course benefited from being able to use stitching machines (sewing machines were first developed in America in the 1840s). Lace-making, the eye-bending and back-bending work of so many very young children as well as cottage women, died out as mass-produced lace became available; the same was true of the covered buttons that were the speciality of some Dorset villages, and of the straw-plaiting practised by countless women and children in cottages all over the land for turning into bonnets and hats. One cottage industry that did persist, and to some extent still does today, was knitting – especially in fishing villages and on the islands. The rates of pay for all these home industries were terrible, so that the hours were appallingly long (often on top of not only housework but probably a bit of farmwork as well), but in hard times the cottage industries contributed substantially and vitally to the family's income and indeed when agricultural unemployment was high the wife and children often supported the household by these occupations. Others made a little money, long into the 20th century, by picking and selling wild produce – daffodils, primroses, violets, blackberries and whortleberries, chequers from the wild service tree, sloes, nuts, mushrooms – or surplus garden produce; others took in washing or needlework, or specialized in the cooking of certain dishes and preserves.

Lace-making was an important cottage industry.

Villages used to have their own trading spinners, dyers and weavers – and sometimes dressmakers and, here and there, village tailors who traditionally sat cross-legged (so that they could spread their work over their laps) in the front window of their cottages as they worked. And they had cobblers to mend boots and shoes, even if they did not have shoe-makers. A good pair of strong boots designed specifically to the individual's foot was essential to every worker.

Most shoe-makers, tailors and cloth-makers were in the towns, catering for those who could afford their services in the days before clothes were mass-produced, but by the end of the 19th century women were beginning to be courted by mail-order companies and men were buying themselves cheap 'slop' suits for Sunday wear, which soon became shabby enough to be

Sunday best for a young
Yorkshire couple outside
their pigeon loft.

working clothes, though more serious labourers wore more appropriate and sturdy outfits – corduroy trousers strapped below the knee, perhaps with white slop jackets in summer – and carried their field dinners in cotton kerchiefs checked in red and white, blue and white, or red with yellow and black. John Smith, whose Wiltshire shanty was described by Richard Jefferies in the 1880s, was typical in his choice of white corduroy working trousers (yellowed by the clay and sand of his ditching labours), gathered under the knee by leather straps, and huge, clumsy boots – his pair weighed seven pounds when clean and had immensely thick soles reinforced with iron at heel and toe.

Arthur Gibbs, the Gloucester village squire's son, waxed lyrical in the 1890s about the good dress sense of 'simple country folk', the result being, he said, that 'the eye is seldom offended in old-fashioned country places by the latest inventions of tailors and hatters and the ridiculous changes in fashion in which the greater part of the civilized world is wont to delight. Here are to be seen no hideous "checks", but plain, honest clothes of corduroy or rough cloth in natural colours; no absurd little curly "billy cocks", but good, strong broad-brimmed hats of black beaver in winter to keep off the rain, and of white straw in summer to keep off the heat. No white satin ties . . . but broad, old-fashioned scarves of many colours or of blue "birdseye" mellowed by age.'

The Rev. Arthur Young gave the following estimate of what it cost to clothe a Suffolk family with five children, all under the age of 12, in 1797:

Man, kersey waistcoat and breeches ....15 shillings
Woman, red gown and two coats 13s 1½d
First boy, waistcoat and breeches ....11 shillings
Second boy, ditto ....8 shillings
First girl, red gown and two coats ....8 shillings
Second girl, ditto ....7 shillings
Third girl, ditto ....5 shillings
32 yards of cloth for the family £1 17s 4d
14 pairs of stockings, ditto £1 0s 0d
Seven pairs of shoes, ditto £1 6s 0d
Seven hats, ditto ....12 shillings

The total of £8 2s 5½d represented about a fifth of the family's entire annual income.

Until the latter half of the 19th century, and in some places up to the Great War, the most common outfit for English country workers had been the smock or round frock, a thoroughly practical garment which lasted a lifetime. A girl would spent many hours smocking a round frock as a

William Churchill,
veteran of the Crimean
War, in his beautifully
smocked roundfrock.

wedding gift for her husband. It was an outer garment of strong, closely woven linen which managed to shed most of the weather, partly by its material and partly its full design: it was made from two whole widths of cloth, with side seams only and cut quite square, its top part shaped by means of smocking pleats back and front. Ideally it would have a wide collar protecting the shoulders; the sleeves were set very low, well off the shoulder, gathered at the setting and again at the wrist. It did not matter which way round the garment was worn – back and front were the same. The colours were usually white, olive green, dark or light grey – depending on local custom, and the decoration might reflect the wearer's occupation. For example, milkmaids often incorporated heart designs in the smocking, and were still wearing such frocks in late Victorian times. Earlier in the 19th century, women field workers commonly wore round frocks too but by the 1880s they usually wore linsey-woolsey (a coarse linen-and-wool

111

mixture) dresses in winter, or cotton ones in summer, with corduroy gaiters in rough weather and nailed, metal-tipped boots only a little less cumbersome than the men's.

Men would keep a 'best' round frock for Sunday, to be worn with a tall beaver hat or a felt hat, though many would wear their wedding suit on Sundays, which lasted a lifetime. Arthur Beckett, writing in 1908, described an old Sussex cottager wearing his round frock in church with a pair of hedging gloves, a pair of sheepskin gaiters, and a 'wide-awake' hat with a string tied round the crown instead of a hatband. Even in the first years of the 20th century older farmworkers on weekdays wore thick corduroy suits, summer and winter – it was an everlasting material – but by then the younger men preferred Sunday suits of light-coloured cloth, and collars with bright ties instead of the traditional woollen neck scarf.

At work, some still wore the traditional garb of their trade as the century turned, such as the smith's leather apron or the carpenter's thick white baize or felt jacket with an apron and a paper cap, while gypsies still sported red kerchiefs and, yes, those big gold earrings. In the field, straw hats protected the harvesters, and at other times they tended to wear the traditional soft black felt hat, though in the early years of the 20th century field workers began to wear caps instead. Felt hats had so much more character, though: they were worn in all weathers and then chucked on to a nail to dry into random droopy shapes.

Gertrude Jekyll, born in the 1840s, decided that it was in about 1860 that the old country dress breathed its last. She could remember, just, an old man in his Sunday kneebreeches, buckled shoes, high-collared coat and low-crowned beaver hat, wearing a pigtail in the 1850s, and an old woman invariably in a short-sleeved gown under a blue-checked apron and big mob cap. However, by then the young Gertrude usually saw women wearing print gowns and aprons, occasionally with a loose, open-fronted print jacket, with lilac-coloured cotton print sun-bonnets or plain straw bonnets tied under the chin with a ribbon, and short handkerchief-shawls over their shoulders, replaced on Sundays and in winter by large, plain woollen shawls. For haymaking they would, like Thomas Hardy characters, wear linen sun-bonnets with big flaps to avoid sunstroke. Shawls and kerchiefs were perhaps more common in the north of the country, and large, cover-all pinnies in the south-west, while clean white aprons were a trade mark of women who sold their cottage produce in the market-place.

Sunday best was important. Cottage women in Jekyll's part of the country were particularly proud of their black satin Sunday bonnets and their prayer-books wrapped in white hankies with sprigs of sweet herbs between the pages. The daily indoor headwear (also worn under the Sunday black satin) was a cap of white muslin, its pleated border edged with coarse lace to frame the face, and tied with a ribbon over the cap and under the chin, keeping the hair clean and out of the way. Some would use a cotton kerchief as a headscarf in the continental fashion.

They made their own cotton sun-bonnets in quite an elaborate way. The front, several inches deep, was made separately with closely worked rows of plain cording. This was trimmed with pleated frilling 'put in full, facing

Elderly bonneted hop-picker, ready for sun or rain.

forward and ending in a cording at its back' which, according to Jekyll, 'has a more various and richer appearance than that of the front, as it is done "full" instead of plain. There are three such lines of "fulled" frilling and cording, then three more rows of cording, separated by a small space, something less than half-an-inch. Then comes the back, which is formed of the downward gathering together of the stuff to join the top of the curtain.' This curtain protected the wearer's nape and shoulders from the sun. Its upper edge was gathered into the lower edge of the bonnet itself, perhaps with a flat bow.

Straw bonnets involved several manufacturing stages. The straw was plaited into lengths by any member of a cottage household whose hands were otherwise idle for a moment – you could plait as you walked to school or to work in the fields, for example. Plaiting was piecework and was usually collected by a village agent to be sold on to bonnet makers, who in the English style spiralled the plaits in layers that overlapped like the planks on a ship or a barn, sewing through them with needle and thread to hold them in place. William Cobbett, keen to encourage straw bonnet-making as a source of income for cottagers, investigated American and Italian methods – especially the latter, as bonnets from Leghorn were being imported in huge quantities in the early 19th century and threatened to deprive cottagers of their industry. Leghorn hats and bonnets were not overlapped; the circlings of plait were 'knitted' (laid edge to edge) and so neatly and snugly that it was difficult to see the joins.

In that period, a typical cottage woman working in the fields as well as in her own home might wear a felt hat as well as various bonnets or her cottage cap. She might hope to own a petticoat or two of flannel or linsey-woolsey, a linen shift, a gown of 'common stuff' (woven from wool) or a cotton print in summer, a kerchief at her throat, a coarse working apron or a white or checked cotton one, home-knitted stockings and flat shoes or leather boots or pattens. Pattens were common country footwear until the mid 19th century: they were wooden clogs supported on oval iron hoops to lift you above the ubiquitous mud, leaving sharp prints along the footpaths. They had leather toe-pieces and another band of leather tied over the instep with a short lace.

CHILDHOOD

Early Victorian children cut their hair short, whether boys or girls, until they were eight or nine years old. Both sexes wore round, black hats made of coarse felt and wore short sleeves in almost any weather. Younger boys often wore their sisters' cast-offs and it could be difficult to tell boys from

girls at that age. Older girls wore cotton print frocks in summer, stuff frocks in winter, invariably under a long pinafore and with perhaps a plain bonnet; boys wore short round-frocks (known as gabardines) over corduroy suits.

Toys? Not a lot! Cottage children were adept at entertaining themselves. Harking back to his Lakeland boyhood in the 1880s, Ernest Turnbull described all manner of schoolyard games such as Tig (and its varieties, Tig and run in, Tiggy touchwood, Prison bars or Prisoner's base) and Chivy, a game involving dens at opposite corners of the village crossroads and chases down the road crying 'Chivy!' A more complicated version was known as Cosolary: a boy stood in the middle of a rectangular space trying to catch the others as they sprinted from one end to the other – his aim was to hold his captive quite still and clap him on the crown of the head.

Then there was Booly, or Double Duck. Bools were nicely rounded cobble stones, one of which was placed on a mound or large stone known as the Duck, and everybody else hurled their own boolies at it. If they missed, they tried to retrieve their ammunition without being tigged; if they scored a hit and knocked the duck booly off its perch, the owner of the original had to replace it without being tigged himself.

Hatty involved hats or caps, arranged against a wall. One player chucked a ball towards them. If it managed to fall into a hat, its owner rushed to scoop up the ball and then threw it at his scattering friends. Whoever was hit by the ball took his turn at tossing it into the hats and this game could become quite rough!

A ball was also central to the game of Ickly, Ackly, Aiko. This was best played in a farmyard with a long cowshed which could be approached from either side quite freely so that it separated two teams. A team threw the ball over the building, yelling 'ickly ackly aiko'. If a member of the opposing team managed to 'kep' the ball, he charged round the building to hurl it at the opposition – by hitting someone with the ball before it bounced, he gained a prisoner.

Kick Stean was a mixture of blind man's buff and hide-and-seek. Sticky Knife was a potentially lethal game: boys knelt in a small circle on the grass and each in turn stuck his knife into the turf – first by dropping it straight down, then by putting it flat on the ground, point outwards, and flipping the handle over quickly. Then they all tried again while standing, and by dropping the knife over the shoulder, the climax being the difficult test of sticking the knife into the ground and striking it sharply with your hand so that it flew out of the ground, spun through the air and landed point down in the ground again a few yards away . . .

And of course there was Louping – leapfrogging – chanting a familiar series of nonsense words with each leap ('Tuppeny, Nippeny, Spanish fly', for example). And marbles. And tip-cat, a summer game played with a stick for a bat and a piece of rounded wood, pointed at each end, as the cat, in a mixture of cricket and baseball in which you were allowed three strikes at the cat before being out. The scoring involved measuring rather than running: the pitcher judged the number of strides he needed to cover the ground between a circle and where the cat had landed. This simple game was known in India as gullidanda-khelna.

Most popular of all was Minny Cuddy, or mount the cuddy, which seemed to be a mixture of rugger and leapfrog. One team, having lost the toss, bent down in a formal arrangement: one stood with his back to a wall, the next bent over facing him with his head level with the first's waist and clasping him for support; the rest bent down in a similar manner, clasping the hips of the one in front of them. Then each boy in the other team took a running jump, in turn, on to the bending backs until the whole team was on top of its opposition, whereupon they uttered their local chants. The underdogs had to bear the weight until the chant was complete, or they remained underdogs. An article on this game, published in *The Countryman* in 1946, attracted memories not only from all over Britain but also from Canada and India, and the readers offered a superb selection of alternative names for the game: high cockalorum, jump tiddly wagtail, cork the bottle dummy standing, dolly on the mopstick, inkamauns, hucky duck, skin the rabbit, cork the baby's bottle, knuckle grinders, tons of bricks, eagle's claws, buck-buck, bung the barrel – and many more. The readers also supplied equally colourful names for marbles (stonny-gogs, spangie, kypie, dumps, chub, chucket hole, pinkers, spans and snops, for example) and for Tig including hunt the tod, hornygeegle-gaggle, stagarino, tiggy catchin'olt and kickpost-wallney. They remembered a self-explanatory game called strap arse, games involving the use of hazel rods to flick clay pellets into tins or throwing buttons and fishing them back again with wet thumbs, or the highly dangerous game of baste-the-bear (the 'bear' sat on a fence holding one end of a rope, with his 'master' holding the other, while the rest of the gang tried to hit the bear with their knotted handkerchiefs without being touched by the master, who at the same time had to hold on to his end of the rope and avoid pulling his bear off the fence) and war games like Romans and English. There were night-time games of hide-and-seek known as Tackie roon the rucks or Dickie show a light (the 'hare' in this game ran off with an oil lamp, ten minutes ahead of the pack, showing the light briefly to guide them – though they usually managed to follow the smell of the oil as much as the sight of the light). Of course there was hopscotch, and knuckle-bones and spillikins, and many rhyming and skipping games, usually played by girls or younger children. Most of these village games go back many, many centuries but very few are still played now. The children of yesterday had no need for television.

COMMUNICATIONS

The 18th century cottager had little enough time or energy for leisure pursuits and the same was true for much of the 19th. But as the Victorian period wore on, huge social changes were taking place which not only gave more opportunity for something other than work, eat, sleep, but also stimulated an avid interest in the world beyond the village for perhaps the first time in its history. The great improvement in communications lay at the heart of it all – communications which included, above all, transport facilities, the dissemination of news and education.

That schooling became so much more organized, and indeed eventually compulsory, later in the 19th century meant that far, far more cottagers and their children could read and write. And, boy, did they read! They read avidly – they read the advertisements which began to appear in village shop windows for branded goods, and they were persuaded that they wanted those goods. They read daily newspapers, weekly provincials and journals, many of them lying around in the village clubhouse or pub, brought from the cities by the village carrier or by post from emigrant relatives in distant Australia and America – especially the United States. Regular railway users like farmers bought papers at the station and handed them on to their workers so that they found their way into the cottages, in bits or in bundles, and eventually into the privy, where they were read again and again before being put to a baser use. Earlier in the century Cobbett's stirring diatribes had been read aloud at informal gatherings; now the cottagers could read tracts and leaflets for themselves.

Reading the papers was like listening to gossip on a grand scale. But they also read books – they positively hungered for books. Richard Jefferies described it aptly in *The Awakening*:

'Four hundred years after the first printed book was sent out by Caxton the country has begun to read. An extraordinary reflection that twelve generations should pass away presenting the impenetrable front of indifference to the printing-press! The invention which travelled so swiftly from shore to shore till the remote cities of Mexico, then but lately discovered, welcomed it, for four centuries failed to enter the English counties. This incredible delay must not be supposed to be due to any exceptional circumstances or to inquisitorial action. The cause is found in the agricultural character itself . . . the will was wanting. There was no prejudice, for no people admired learning more than the village people, or gave it more willing precedence. It was simple indifference, which was mistaken for lack of intelligence, but it was most certainly nothing of the kind. How great, then, must be the change when at last, after four hundred years, the country begins to read!'

Books, he claimed, had been available even in rural areas for those who persisted in tracking them down; but too many cottagers were unaware of them, let alone had the cunning and time to find them. However, in Jefferies's own time the situation was changing fast, and then: 'To read everything and anything! The cottagers in far-away hamlets, miles from a railway station, read every scrap of printed paper that drifts across their way, like leaves in autumn. The torn newspapers in which the grocer at the market town wraps up their weekly purchases, stained with tallow or treacle, are not burned heedlessly. Some paragraph, some fragment of curious information, is gathered from the pieces. The ploughman at his luncheon reads the scrap of newspaper in which his bread-and-cheese was packed for him. Men read the bits of paper in which they carry their screws of tobacco. The stone-pickers in spring in the meadows, often women, look at the bits of paper scattered here and there before putting them in their baskets. A line here and a line younder, one to-day, one to-morrow, in time make material equal to a book.'

With reading came knowledge, and an urge to know more and more. Jefferies noted that the eagerness to read newspapers seemed to erupt during the 1870s. But what of books? How did a cottager get hold of them? It was a problem. Pedlars began to sell pamphlets, ballad sheets, dream books, almanacs, small monographs and narrative tales – and country people particularly relished tales of the sea and shipwrecks, it seems. The pedlar also offered a small selection of religious essays and weekly romantic novelettes, often no more than pages stitched together without any cover. Gypsies, too, began to sell similar publications along with their clothes-pegs. The village shop or post office, however, was not a good source: it might sell stationery to letter-writers and provincial newspapers but only the occasional child's book. You had to go to a town, where you might be lucky enough to find a few second-hand books on archaeology in an odds-and-ends shop. In larger market towns (those with good railway stations) you might fare better for choice if you had the money for nicely bound books costing from five to ten shillings apiece, or if you had a taste for 'good' novels or for educational manuals. The latter did not appeal to cottagers: they were pretty fed up with Victorian do-gooders telling them how to do things anyway.

So the book-loving cottager was easily frustrated. A Londoner was spoilt for choice, but a villager . . .

Jefferies realized that villagers received no knowledge of what the publishers were by then pouring out in thousands of new titles every year, nor could they afford them even if they did know about them. Anyway, many failed to meet their taste. What a villager would have asked for, if he had been aware that it might exist, would *not*, said Jefferies, be 'something written in the plainest language, specially chosen, as words of one syllable are for children. What is designed for the village must not be written down to it. The village will reject rice and corn-flour – it will only accept strong meat.' They wanted something strong in subject, strong in manner, powerfully written. They would love to read travellers' tales in particular, opening their eyes to amazing new worlds in which they could still recognize their own struggles with the land and nature – they could imagine themselves in the traveller's situation. And battles with big game, or graphically portrayed historical battles (the fighting of them, the physical fighting, not the political scheming). And, eagerly, they would read about the 'wonders of science' as long as the tone did not smack of the schoolroom.

So much for content. In practical terms, however, it was a case of what could be afforded. Books needed to be cheap – a florin at most, and preferably no more than a bob each. Americans of the time could buy books for a few cents, and the French for no more than a franc (ten English pennies): they were badly printed on poor paper and had no fancy binding, but it was the text that mattered – words, the meat of the book. Blow the binding! and blow the do-gooders, well-meaning of course but too often censorious, who were busily setting up village reading rooms where worthiness was the word.

Reading rooms were designed for the self-improvement of artisans and workers: they offered further education in the form of lectures and classes, and penny readings by the parson, with perhaps a few well chosen newspapers and journals on the table. Papers and journals were also found in village clubhouses along with the cards and other games.

To give the villagers a better choice of reading material, Jefferies tried to encourage the sale (not loan) of books by travelling libraries. The problem, however, was one of marketing. How could a scattered rural population be made aware that the library was in the area? You could not just ring your bell on the green; and it would take far too much effort, time and expense to go cottage to cottage in the days when most people were out during the day anyway. The travelling bookseller, decreed Jefferies, should regard himself more as a prophet than a businessman: his role should be to open people's eyes to books and then let them create their own demand for them.

Another idea was to sell books to cottagers by mail order – the Reader's Digest approach, if you like. In the 1870s country people received so little post that they eagerly read every word of whatever the postman did bring. 'The arrival of a letter or two is still an event; it is read twice or three times, put in the pocket, and looked at again.' Drapery businesses had already found a very lucrative country market for their mail-order goods; indeed many farmhouses relied almost entirely on mail order for their materials, *and* they could get the very latest fashions from London that way rather than whatever the local town might stock. But that was the bigger houses and farms. 'Cottagers', said Jefferies, 'never receive a circular at all. If a circular came to a cottage by post it would be read and re-read, folded up neatly, and preserved. After a time – for an advertisement is exactly like seed sown in the ground – something would be done. Some incident would happen, and it would be remembered that there was something about it in the circular – some book that dealt with the subject. There is business directly. The same post that brought the original circular, distributing knowledge of books, can bring the book itself.'

Another method of selling books to cottagers might be by putting up posters. This would be a first for booksellers, though auctioneers and others were well aware of the novelty value of a poster in places where most people still used their legs and spent most of the day out of doors. Though posters in London and in towns and railway stations were ubiquitous and unnoticed, in the country they were rare enough to catch the curious eye.

This was still an age in which people left messages for each other at a rendezvous – a lover might chalk a few words on the meadow gate if an assignation could not be kept, or leave a note written on a scrap of paper in a cleft stick pushed into the ground. Oh yes, posters would be read.

Advertisements in local papers would also be read avidly. Country people, in contrast to those in town, read their local paper 'from the title to the printer's address', including all the ads, even the regular ones to make sure that they had not subtly changed since last week. Regularity was important: the bookseller's display needed to be repeated every week to succeed. Country people were slow to act but the drip-drip technique worked.

The essence of Jefferies's long essay on country literature was that the physical presence of books was so commonplace in towns that they were dismissed but so rare in the countryside that they were hugely exciting, but that the publishers seemed to be quite unaware of this vast potential market out in the sticks. (Many still are today . . .) However, it was the *reading* of the books, more than the pride of possessing them, that stirred most cottagers and it was these readers who were at last satisfied by rural lending libraries started by the new county councils just after the First World War. They put books into suitable existing premises in the villages; later they offered the better stocked mobile libraries that even now can be the highlight of the week in many rural areas – partly for the books but partly as a casual social venue for gossip. After all, what is a cottage garden gate for if not gossiping over? And, in a modern age when people are more likely to drive down the lane than walk it, cottage gates have lost that role. Why, the cottager does not even have the other old excuse for a gossip – that of going down the lane to collect a 'handful of fire' from a neighbour's hot embers to re-light the hearth, the old practice before matches were universally available.

All was not lost! During the brief lull between the world's two huge wars in the first half of the 20th century, a new way to gossip began to find its way into cottage homes, very gradually. William Budd, builder, wheelwright and undertaker (a common combination of trades), lived in his Elizabethan cottage in the 1920s in a style more appropriate to the 1880s but was the proud – very proud – possessor of a telephone. It gave him a tremendous sense of superiority and he was really pleased with himself for having the uncharacteristic foresight to appreciate that a telephone was a good business investment, especially for his undertaking. The machine, with a mouth-piece that reminded his young grand-daughter of a large black daffodil, was installed with great ceremony in his dark, gloomy, green-distempered 'office', its bell exciting the whole household every time it rang. Granny was terrified of it, but so she was of electricity and the wireless and motor cars on the roads. 'She had lived her life till she had reached a moment in time which satisifed her, and there, it seemed, she had decided to remain, determined to go no further,' wrote Mavis Budd. No wonder: Granny had survived into times when modern technology was changing everybody's way of life at a far faster rate than ever before, telescoping the natural leisure of time like a film on fast-forward.

The Budds' telephone was indeed a coup. Only the 'better' classes had such marvels in the '20s and even quite prosperous farmers regarded them with extreme distrust and thought them quite unnecessary. (They were saying the same about tractors, and two generations later about computers.) Certainly no ordinary cottagers could afford them, or would have found much use for them. Eric Blair – better known as George Orwell, author of *Nineteen Eighty-four* and *Animal Farm* – had been the first in his own tiny village of Wallington, Hertfordshire, to have a telephone and that was in the late 1930s when his 300-year-old lath-and-plaster cottage was half given over to being a village stores. He was making about thirty bob a week in takings, keeping an eye out for customers through four slits he had cut out of the door that connected his living-room shop with the study in which he smoked and wrote all day. He still had an outdoor privy then, and no gas or electricity.

The telephone had been invented long before but the public kiosks and post-office instruments which began to appear in some villages during the '20s and '30s would be the only telephones that most villagers would use until after the Second World War. Family news from distant parts continued to be relayed by post, in a time (quite unlike our own) when handwritten envelopes and postcards formed the bulk of the postman's load.

The wireless, however, was accepted with joy and saved up for with great fervour once the BBC's regular public broadcasts began to spread across the nation's airwaves. Before the wireless, news had been received through gossip – word-of-mouth between cottagers or from visiting traders, some of whom also brought provincial newspapers. By the 1890s several village shops were depending more on their income from selling newspapers than from provisions.

The late Victorian period opened the cottager's eyes to the world beyond the village, the world beyond England too, and the new means of communication were not solely for receiving second-hand reports. People began to travel and see for themselves as well. Before, cottagers had *walked*, which limited their travels in the constraints of time and energy. The rapid spread of the railway network from the mid 19th century onwards eventually benefited cottagers, once there were enough local stations to be within walking distance of home and once the passenger fares had become more affordable, but far more liberating was the bicycle, which gave personal independence and virtually free travelling once the machine had been purchased.

During the 1920s in particular, the country bus came into its own to add to the cottager's choice of transport, often right to the cottage door, which was much more convenient and friendly than the train. In many cases a local service was run by village carriers who had swapped their horses and carts for motors, and many a soldier returning from the Great War set up as a village's busman, perhaps living in one of the 'homes for heroes' built with the encouragement of a grateful government. The old cottages were not good enough for men who had survived the hell of the Great War.

Yes, Granny Budd's world had changed radically during her lifetime. Not long after her diamond wedding anniversary, Ellen Matilda Budd (née Wells) quietly decided she had had enough of it all. She was not ill, nor was she unhappy, but in the early hours of one morning she felt 'queer', took a sip of brandy, told her family, 'I be going ter die,' calmly closed her eyes and did so. Somehow, the era of the real cottagers died with her.

BIBLIOGRAPHY

Ayres, James, *The Shell Book of the Home in Britain* (Faber & Faber, London, 1981)

Ayto, Eric G., *Clay Tobacco Pipes* (Shire, 2nd ed., Aylesbury, 1987)

Baxter, J., *Baxter's Library of Agricultural & Horticultural Knowledge* (J. Baxter, Lewes, 1834)

Beckett, Arthur, *The Spirit of the Downs* (Methuen, London, 1909)

Blum, Jerome (ed.), *Our Forgotten Past* (Thames & Hudson, London, 1982)

Brunskill, R.W., *Illustrated Handbook of Vernacular Architecture* (Faber & Faber, London, 1971)

Budd, Mavis, *Dust to Dust* (J.M. Dent & Sons, London, 1966)

Cobbett, William, *Cottage Economy* (1823, reprinted Landsman, Bromyard, 1974)

Creaton, David, *The Beasts of my Fields* (Hodder & Stoughton, London, 1977)

Eveleigh, David J., *Candle Lighting* (Shire, Aylesbury, 1985) *Firegrates and Kitchen Ranges* (Shire, Aylesbury, 1982) *Old Cooking Utensils* (Shire, Aylesbury, 1986)

Fussell, G.E. & K.R., *The English Countrywoman* (Bloomsbury, London, 1985)

Gibbs, J. Arthur, *A Cotwold Village, or, Country Life and Pursuits in Gloucestershire* (Jonathan Cape, London, 1898)

Gledhill, David, *Gas Lighting* (Shire, Aylesbury, 1981)

Hammond, Martin, *Bricks and Brickmaking* (Shire, Aylesbury, 2nd ed., 1990)

Hardyment, Christina, *From Mangle to Microwave, The Mechanization of Household Work* (Polity Press, Cambridge, 1990)

Harris, Richard, *Discovering Timber-Framed Buildings* (Shire, Aylesbury, 2nd ed., 1979)

Hartley, Dorothy, *The Land of England* (Macdonald, London, 1979)

Horn, Pamela (ed.), *Oxfordshire Village Life: The Diaries of George James Dew (1846-1928), Relieving Officer* (Beacon Publications, Sutton Courtenay, 1983)

Iredale, David, and John Barrett, *Discovering Your Old House* (Shire, 3rd ed., Aylesbury, 1991)

Jefferies, Richard, *The Toilers of the Field* (Longmans Green, London, 1892)

Jekyll, Gertrude, *Old West Surrey* (Longmans Green, London, 1904)

Jekyll, Gertrude, and Sydney R. Jones, *Old English Household Life* (1925)

Jones, Sydney R., *English Village Homes* (Batsford, London, 1936)

Mingay, G.E., *Rural Life in Victorian England* (Alan Sutton, Stroud, 1990)

Mitford, Mary Russell, *Our Village* (first published 1824-32)

Pingriff, G.N., *Leicestershire* (Cambridge University Press, Cambridge, 1920)

Pitt, W., *General View of the Agriculture of the County of Worcester* (1813)

Powell, Christopher, *Discovering Cottage Architecture* (Shire, Aylesbury, 1984)

Pulbrook, Ernest C., *English Country Life and Work* (Batsford, London, 1922)

Reid, Richard, *The Shell Book of Cottages* (Michael Joseph, London, 1977)

Reyburn, Wallace, *Flushed with Pride: The Story of Thomas Crapper* (Macdonald, London, 1969)

Smith, Anne (ed.), *The Victorian House Catalogue, Young & Marten* (Sidgwick & Jackson, London, 1990)

Smith, Frederick, and Barbara Wilcox, *Living in the Country* (A & C Black, London, 1941)

Vancouver, Charles, *General View of the Agriculture of the County of Devon* (1808)

Woodforde, John, *The Truth about Cottages* (Routledge & Kegan Paul, London, 1969)

Young, Rev. Arthur, *General View of the Agriculture of the County of Sussex* (1813)

INDEX

ADVERTISEMENTS 75, 122
Ailments 88–90
Allingham, Mrs Helen 8, 81

BACON 43, 56, 81
Baconlofts 12, 42
Baking 42, 49–50
Baths 64–5, 72
Bats 77
Baxter of Lewes 83, 84, 88, 90
Bays 13
Beds/bedding 99, 103–6
Bees 79
Besoms 75
Bicycles 123
Birds 30, 46, 78
Boilers 47, 48, 73
Boil-in-a-bag 44–5
Bonfires 74
Bonnets 112–4
Books 118–22
Bread 42, 84
Brewing 58
Bricks 12, 17, 19, 22, 36
Brushwood 17, 34, 36
Budd, Mavis 59–60, 70, 76-7,
  106, 122–4
Building materials 16–26
Bundling 105

CANDLES 52, 54–5, 69
Carpets 36, 37, 75
Cesspits: see Sanitation
Chickens 74, 79
Children 37, 69, 114–7
Chimney cranes 41, 45, 47
Chimneys 12, 19, 28, 29, 46
Clay pipes 101
Cleaning 74–5
Clocks 98–9
Clothes 37, 106–14
Cob 18, 20, 22, 25
Cobbett, William 26, 52, 53, 57,
  83–4, 102, 114, 118
Cockroaches 77, 89
Colour 94–5, 103
Commonland 25, 31, 81

Communications 117–124
Cooking 40-49
Copper (washing) 11, 48, 61–3,
  64
Cottage industries 52, 107
Cows 21, 22, 79
Creaton, David 70
Crockery 97
Cupboards 14, 102–3

DAMP 36, 38
Dating 17, 25
Daub 17, 18, 28, 30
Defoe, Daniel 16, 30
Dew, George 56, 58, 65–6, 78
Disease 27, 65–6
Doors 34
Draughts 38, 40, 46, 100–101
Dressers 14, 97, 103

EARTH CLOSETS: see Privies
Elder 30, 86–7, 89
Electricity 56–51, 73, 75
Enamelware 51, 97

FAT 52, 53, 57, 97
Feathers 75, 106
Fireplaces 12, 13, 26–8, 40–50
Fleas 78, 89
Flies 78
Flooding 20, 36
Floors 14, 25, 30, 35–7
Flowers 90–92
French, Mary 49
Fruit 88
Fuel 46, 47
Furniture 27, 99–101, 102–3

GAMES 115–7
Gardens 10, 21, 22, 30, 81–92
Gas 50–51, 56
Gibbs, Arthur 110
Glass/glazing 14, 31, 32–3
Glove-making 52, 107
Goats 79

HEADWEAR 112–4

Hearths 13, 27
Herbs 88–90
Hexam, Lizzie 27
Horsehair 18, 36, 105–6

ICE 57
Idlebacks 45
Inglenooks 40, 46, 101
Insects 30, 77, 78, 89
Ironing 62

JEFFERIES, Richard 8, 30, 77, 78,
  88, 99, 101, 118–22
Jekyll, Gertrude 8, 54, 91, 102,
  112
Jones, Sydney 10, 71

KETTLES 45–6
Knitting 107

LACE-MAKING 52, 107
Larders 56
Latches 34
Laundry 61–5
Lawrence, Emily 44, 46, 67
Lewis, Mrs 63–4
Libraries 124
Lighting 27, 52–6
Limewash 20, 94–5
Loudon, John Claudius 37, 82

MANTELL, J. 91
M.E.R.L. 63, 64
Medicines 58
Mitford, Mary 91–2
Mud (see also Daub) 16, 17–19,
  20, 22

NETTLES 11, 70
Newspapers 118

OIL LAMPS 56
Oil stoves 51
Old Pound Cottage 13–15, 32
Orchards 22, 88
Ornaments 97–8
Orwell, George 123

127

Outshuts 12, 13
Ovens 12, 42, 47, 49

PADLEY, Nellie 31
Paint 36, 94–5
Parlours 12, 37–9
Pictures 38, 68, 95
Pigs 21, 52, 56, 74, 78, 79–81
Plaster 17, 18, 28, 30, 35, 36
Plumbing 71, 72–3
Potatoes 21, 22, 52, 82–5
Preserves 56–7
Privies 11, 65, 66–70
Pumps 22, 59–60, 61

QUETHIOCK 49

RANGES 39, 47–50, 73
Reading 117–22
Recycling 37, 73–4, 106–7
Redware 61, 97
Refrigeration 56, 57
Remedies 88–90
Rodents 30, 60, 77, 78
Roof 12, 13, 14, 17
Roundfrocks 110–12

Rubbish 11, 35, 73–4
Rushes 17, 34, 36, 37, 52–4, 100

SANITATION 27, 36, 65–73
Septic tanks/sewage: see Sanitation
Sideboards 14, 99
Sinks 11, 61
Sleeping lofts 12, 27, 29, 104
Smocks 110–2
Smoke 13–14, 27, 28, 31, 38, 49
Songhurst 9–13
Spits 14, 41–2
Squatters 28, 31
Stairs 12, 14, 29
Stone 17, 19, 22, 36
Stoneware 97
Stools 46, 99
Straw 18, 20, 34, 35, 36, 100, 105–6, 107

TEA 46, 83
Telephones 122–3
Thatch 17, 20
Tiles 17, 20, 36
Tinderbox 55
Transport 123

Turf 18, 20
Typhoid 65–6

UPSTAIRS 29–30

VEGETABLE CROPS 86
Ventilation 33, 38

WALLPAPER 95
Washing 61–4
Water 11, 22, 58–61, 70–71, 72
Wattles 13, 17, 18, 28, 30, 34
Wells 11, 58–61
Whitewash 22, 95
Wickerwork 100, 103
Wilcox, Barbara 38, 60
Wildlife 32, 76–8
Wild plants 88–9
Windows 12, 31–4
Wine-making 58, 65
Wireless 123
Wooden utensils 96–7

YEW TREES 11, 68
Young, Arthur 20, 110